The
Dash to
Significance

CAROL,
Nope you find a
few nuggers that
will enrich your 'DASH'

Bob

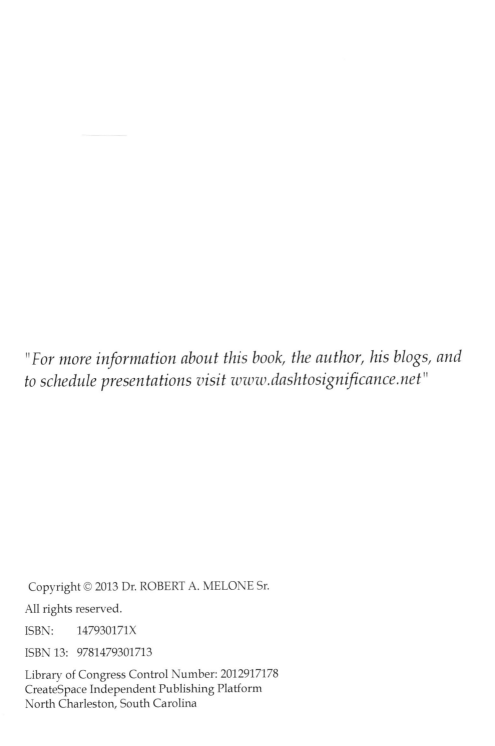

"For more information about this book, the author, his blogs, and to schedule presentations visit www.dashtosignificance.net"

ISBN: 147930171X

ISBN 13: 9781479301713

Library of Congress Control Number: 2012917178
CreateSpace Independent Publishing Platform
North Charleston, South Carolina

Dedicated to my wife, Juanita, our kids Bob (Jeanne), Tim (Lucinda),Karyn (Tom), Kelli (Dave) and their children, Stefan, Jacob, Kirsten, Jordan, Alyssa, Kara, Aimee, Jonah, Kelsey, Zachary, Alyvia, Leah and Judah Moses. Thanks for your love in my dash to significance.

The
Dash to
Significance

A Guide to Living a Fulfilling Life

DR. ROBERT A. MELONE SR.

Table of Contents

CHAPTER 1

Introduction

I arise in the morning torn between a desire to improve the world and a desire to enjoy the world. This makes it hard to plan the day.

— ELWYN BROOKS WHITE

Checking the obituary page is not a daily routine, but one day something caught my eye, and I began to look at the pictures of the deceased and to read the stories of their lives. Their lives were depicted with characterizations such as:

- He was a US Army veteran of Vietnam, serving with the Eighty-Second Airborne and Special Forces unit.
- She was an inspiration of strength and courage during her journey with cancer.
- A graduate of Apex College, she retired from the South Carolina Department of Corrections division with over thirty years of service.
- She enjoyed cooking for her family and friends.
- He was a member of the American Legion in Cary.
- He lived his forty-one years to the fullest, with honor, integrity, dedication, and service to those he loved. He reminded us each and every day to love and cherish our families and friends.

As I continued to skim the events of their lives, I began to reflect on how my own obituary might read. What will they say about me? None of us know when we will die. Some would suggest that if we knew the "when" and "where" of our lives, this would somehow improve the days we have left. But any one of us, if he or she wishes, may select his or her own epitaph. I immediately began to reflect on my own life and thought about my degrees, my successes, and my accomplishments. All those plaques on my library wall. The clubs I served in for so many years. I thought about all my achievements, those activities that had brought pride to my life. But then I recalled a day recently when I decided to take down some of the "trophies" on my wall—my college diplomas, awards, recognitions, and other symbols of my successes. For some reason they had lost some of their meaning.

Like most young men now in their fifties and sixties, I had rushed through college, found the love of my life, embarked on a career, climbed the corporate ladder, and acquired many of the things we believe to be the American symbols of success. At some point, one that is different for everyone, we begin to ask, "Is this really as good as it gets?" But something drives us to buy a newer car, a bigger house, trips to the shore, more toys—toys that never satisfy us and fail to provide the thrill they once did. We question the meaning of life, our lives in particular; the inevitability of death begins to close in on us more frequently. And while we may not necessarily fear the end of the game of life, we want to be sure we "finish well." Depending on our circumstances, "well" can be defined in many ways—spiritually, physically, materially, financially, emotionally. Or in whatever other capacity we may use to measure the wellness of our lives.

At some point during this personal reflection, I was introduced to a great paperback, *Halftime: Moving from Success to Significance* by Bob Buford. This book challenged me to discover the difference between success and significance. Buford suggests that the first half of our lives is a quest for success, whereas the second half is a journey toward significance. While you may not fear the end of the game, you do want to make sure you leave something behind that no one can take away from you—not just some monetary inheritance but rather something that will be carried in the hearts and minds of those you leave behind.[1]

Where are you in your quest for success? Is success still your goal, or is significance your focus? Many of you are still in your thirties or early forties and feel the full impact of the challenge of trying to achieve success. You may be

---

1   Bob Buford, *Halftime: Moving from Success to Significance* (Grand Rapids, MI: Zondervan, 1994), 43.

looking for a promotion or trying to make that extra sale so you can make the mortgage payment on a house you really don't need. Or maybe you want a garage full of toys to play with during increased leisure time, new clothes, or cosmetic surgery. What drives you? Peer pressure—that unfulfilled need that is never satisfied? Regardless of the underlying motive, let's call it the quest for success.

In their book *One Month to Live*, Kerry and Chris Shook refer to this stage as the "motion sickness of our souls."[2] Even though we live at a rushed pace, we begin to experience this motion sickness—always moving to the next big thing, trying to satisfy something in ourselves. We think, *If I can just change my looks, if I can change my house or my car, then it's going to change me. Then I will truly be content.* There is only one problem: it doesn't work!

Many of you are playing in the third and fourth quarters of your lives. For you it's time to realize most of the game has already been played. Maybe it's time now to call a time-out and stop the clock, to huddle up and think about reaffirming your game plan—a plan that moves you from success to significance. This will be a plan that dares you to believe that what you ultimately leave behind will be more important than anything you could have achieved in the first half of your life. A plan that includes the changes you've been thinking about making someday or the fences you've been meaning to mend—actions that need to be done. *Now.*

Don't end up in a too-little, too-late situation—beginning to be a better parent, spouse, Christian, community member, friend…but too late. It's time to begin believing that work is

---

2 Kerry Shook and Chris Shook, *One Month to Live: Thirty Days to a No-Regrets Life* (Colorado Springs, CO: Waterbrook, 2008), 144.

a living, not a life. Maybe: You still have time to recall the vision and ambitions of your youth and be the person you always wanted to be. Now you can do the experiences that really bring meaning to your life — things more significant than those awards collecting dust on your library walls that nobody looks at any more. It's never too late to take your strengths, knowledge, and experiences and weave them into a mosaic of significance, a mosaic that not only gives your life meaning but also influences the lives of those around you.

One of the best daily reminders for many of us, a life-altering experience for some and a way of life for others, is the poem "The Dash" by Linda Ellis.[3] Ellis uses the dash on your tombstone between birth and death as an illustration of how your life is represented. Each of us is given our own personal dash, the importance of making it count will never be greater.

Reading the poem reminded me that living a dash doesn't mean trying to be perfect or changing yourself to fit the mold of what people tend to think of as a "good" person. Rather, it means doing the best you can every day to live a life that may someday allow you to leave behind a legacy of kindness, love, laughter, and fullness — a legacy that will endure. In the end, our true worth and significance come not from what we have accomplished or attained but in the legacy we leave in the hearts and minds of those we've loved and who've loved us.

In the pages that follow are my thoughts dedicated to assisting you to live your life to the fullest by living

---

3   Linda Ellis, "The Dash," Retrieved from http://lindaellis.net/the-dash-poem-by-linda-ellis/.

passionately and purposefully, the way God created you to live. You will be reminded that our time on earth is limited and that during this limited time we are all challenged to live significantly and, through our actions, to magnify the significance of each life we touch.

CHAPTER 2

Success vs. Significance

*We make a living by what we get, but we make
a life by what we give.*

— WINSTON CHURCHILL

When my father was born in 1905, few people lived beyond what we now consider middle age. As late as 1929, average life expectancy in the United States was not even fifty years, and a half century earlier, it was around thirty-five years. But today a great majority of Americans can expect to live twice as long as their grandparents did.

7

With such short lives, achieving the success their child-hood potential indicated was difficult, if not impossible, for people. The combined years of education or training, plus developing a skill or trade, left little time for thinking about success and a meaningful life, even in those days. The focus was more on sustenance than on success. These individuals, who were mainly manual workers, were ready to retire after thirty years. They wouldn't miss their work. Work was generally a means to an end, a way to put food on the table or new shoes on their feet.

Especially after World War II, large numbers of workers began to explore new ways of being successful and finding meaning in their lives: something that had been an unknown quantity in the past. Success in these years didn't necessarily mean fame or fortune, but it did mean greater opportunities to enjoy their work, to financially improve their lives, or to increase their potential for personal fulfillment.

As our country matured economically, larger segments of our society were freed from the tediousness of their work lives and were able to enjoy more of life's comforts — bigger houses, more luxurious automobiles, higher education, leisure activities, and the accumulation of wealth. For some, success became earning a college degree, landing a great job, and having a house with a white picket fence, a spouse, and two and a half kids who attended a private school. A job with a VP title, a six-figure income, and a membership in a prestigious private club became more common aspirations and were within the reach of many. These achievements became the American symbols of the "good life."

But as many achieved these aspirations, we began to realize that the problem with this rationale was that success was fleeting; it comes, it goes, but ultimately it doesn't satisfy us very long. Our culture has a way of asking, "What are your *recent* successes?" Americans began to notice that even when they accomplished something of worth, the joy of the accomplishment disappeared rather quickly. Eventually we came to realize that our struggles were not with success but with significance.

Success versus significance: some would say any discussion along these lines is nothing more than a semantic debate. The sad reality is that far too many people either confuse success with significance or are so focused on success that they are actually blind to the meaning of significance.

Look around and you'll see that many people use their knowledge, resources, and experiences to acquire things in an attempt to satisfy their personal desires, which, in their minds, constitute success. Contrast this with people who use their knowledge, resources, and experiences to serve and benefit others, a strategy that, by most standards, constitutes significance.

For many, success begins and ends with the achievement of a certain list of personal goals, with little regard to their impact on others. These people confuse success with significance, and, regardless of their wealth and professional accomplishments, they won't accomplish true greatness, which comes only through making significant contributions to something other than themselves. Too often success for many has an expiration date and depends on winning the next "trophy" to maintain the sense of accomplish-ment. Because of this, we can never really be free if this is the main gauge by which we assess and measure our lives. Significance is more about a central thread or theme that runs through our lives and supports our choices. It is about meaning and purpose.

General Douglas MacArthur once said, "A man doesn't grow old because he has lived a certain number of years; he grows old when he deserts his ideals. The years may wrinkle your skin, but deserting your ideals wrinkles your soul." Our souls often become wrinkled if we focus only on the successes of life. A long-standing myth about success and significance says that having one automatically excludes the other. For instance, many people believe that if they are successful and have other abundant gifts, then significance, meaning, and happiness must somehow be forfeited. On the flip side, an equally widely-held belief is that if they somehow "break the code" and manifest significance and happiness in their life-times, then success will play only a minor role in their lives.

The question each of us must ask ourselves as we con-tinue to grow inwardly is this: Is how I'm living my life leading to success or significance? Success is usually what we get on the way up the ladder of life. It's what we've been striving for. But we often get to a certain point and find that this link of success no longer really matters.

Did you ever get something you really wanted only to find that it was not as satisfying as you thought it would be? In *Seeds of Success*, Bill and Billy Moyer suggest that this attitude "starts early in our lives. As children, we cannot sleep on Christmas Eve. What's Santa going to bring? And then Christmas morning comes, and it lasts five minutes. You open everything and say, 'What's next?' That's what success is. But it's significance we are seeking; it's not about what we get but rather what we leave behind that matters. No amount of success in the world can trump significance."[4]

George Bernard Shaw once said, "To be used for a purpose recognized by yourself as a mighty one...I am of the opinion that my life belongs to the whole community and as long as I live, it is my privilege to do for it whatever I can. I want to be thoroughly used up when I die, for the harder I work the more I live." This reading caused me to reflect on the ways in which my life is "being used up." What is my metric for measuring my level of significance? Am I making a difference at some level? How about you? Are you making a difference?

The major focus of this work is not to encourage you to select one lifestyle over another, or to choose to live a life of success or significance. Rather, my aim is to share with you the values that have been paramount in allowing me to live a life of greater significance and, by example, to provide my loved ones, friends, and acquaintances a role model for living a more significant life: a lifestyle that allows success and significance to reside side by side. I began by brainstorming a list of important values that have characterized the lives of notable persons. Some live by five major values, some by ten, others by as many as fifteen. Then I challenged myself as to whether these values were evident in my own life. Did they play a role in the significance of my life? Were their roles really important?

---

4 Bill Moyer and Billy Moyer, *Seeds of Success: A Journey from Success to Significance* (Waco, TX: The Leading Edge, 2009), 67.

After much deliberation, I narrowed my list to eight. They are forgiveness, nature, relationships, generosity, integrity, service to others, perseverance, and Christian faith. Even after a tentative commitment to these eight values, I periodically reevaluated my decision and revised the list. My daily commitment to each of these values still often vacillates, but that does not necessarily diminish the overall importance of each value.

Your list may appear very different from mine, and that's OK. After you read the next eight chapters, which describe my most significant values, I'd be interested in learning about the factors that make *your* life one of significance. Even though our lists may be different, I hope we can agree that by using our personalized lists of values, significant lives may leave a legacy. Significance demands that we take the focus off our own pursuits, accomplishments, and possessions, and identify ways in which we can leverage our success for the good of others. But above all, significance requires that we leave this earth a better place than when we entered it. Other lives will be enriched because we took the time to leave a legacy by sharing our experiences with the world.

Exercises That Strengthen Significance

- Have I served my community today, be it locally or globally?
- Have I today given without expectation of receiving?
- Have I done something to take care of my spirit?
- Have I mentored, taught, helped, or coached someone?

- Have I created something that will influence someone else?
- Have I been present and involved with my family?
- Have I been there for my friends and colleagues?
- Have I led with compassion?
- Am I leaving a footprint I'm proud of?
- Have I given anonymously?

CHAPTER 3

Forgiveness

To err is human, to forgive divine.

— ALEXANDER POPE

The Hurts of Our Lives

We are all wounded. Even on our best days, our self-esteem hovers somewhere between feeble and fragile. All it takes is a little disapproval or perceived disapproval to send us staggering. From the time we are young, actions we or others take may create some type of negative emotional memory. For example, a commitment not being kept, hurtful words, betrayal of a confidence, unfulfilled expectations, sexual abuse, or a simple cutoff in traffic can have a negative influence. Examples of events involving only ourselves might include a rush to judgment, a poor financial decision, a poor choice of friends, or a minor decision, such as wearing the wrong dress or suit for that special occasion.

Whatever the issue, these memories create a personal dynamic that continues within us. This trapped dynamic remains in our minds, often becoming a source of disharmony that has the potential to affect our physical bodies or our psychological well-being; feelings of anger, bitterness, and even vengeance may result. We often feel we are drowning in our own negative emotions. Bitterness and resentment feed on themselves, creating an ever-widening circle of despair. "But if we don't practice forgiveness," says Dr. Katherine Piderman at the Mayo Clinic, "we may be the ones who pay most dearly. By embracing forgiveness, we embrace peace, hope, gratitude, and joy."[5] When we forgive, we release this anger and give ourselves permission to be happy.

Why We Don't Forgive

The word *forgiveness* means "to give up resentment against or the desire to punish; stop being angry with, pardon, to give up all claims to punish or exact penalty for (an offense);

---

5 "Forgiveness: Letting Go of Grudges and Bitterness." Mayo Clinic, November 23, 2011, http://www.mayoclinic.com/health/forgiveness/MH00131.

to overlook; to cancel or remit a debt."[6] Forgiveness occurs when an individual who has been hurt or offended gives up his or her desire to avoid the person who hurt him or her, or gives up the desire to exact revenge on that person and also seeks reconciliation with that person if it's safe and possible.

Loretta Lanphier cites the fact that "94 percent of respondents in a national Gallup poll indicated that forgiveness was important, but interestingly, only 48 percent said they usually tried to forgive others."[7] We have a tendency to hold on to our resentment and never give reconciliation a thought. Playing the victim gives us comfort that comes with being right. As the victim, we give ourselves sympathy, which allows us to bask in the righteous anger of a wronged person. The victim's role may seem like a superior option to our injured pride and selfish ego, and in the short term, it gives us the illusory comfort that comes with being in the right. The victim gets all the sympathy and stands on moral high ground. Although "an eye for an eye" often feels most satisfying if we lack the power to deliver actual harm, anger may seem like the next-best choice. In a certain sense holding a grudge does feel good. We want to hold on to our grudges, believing we will lose control if we humble ourselves and grant forgiveness. The anger fuels us. We forget how to function without it and even embrace it because it keeps us going. In reality, just the opposite is true: if we harbor anger in our hearts, we're actually the ones who have lost control and are in bondage to anger.

---

6   *Webster's New World Dictionary*, 3rd college ed., s.v. "forgiveness."

7   Loretta Lanphier, "2010 Health Resolution—Walk in Forgiveness," *Oasis of Health and Wellness* (blog), January 4, 2010, http://www. oasisadvancedwellness.com/health-articles/2010/01/2010-health-resolution-%E2%80%93-walk-in-forgiveness.html.

Often a failure to forgive is a desire to satisfy our sense of justice. Even if we are not angry, we may find ourselves withholding forgiveness to avoid appearing to condone the offense, especially if we believe the one who offended us doesn't deserve our forgiveness. When we don't think forgiveness implies that we condone the injustice committed against us, releasing our anger and forgiving the offender may feel like letting him get away without being punished, especially if no other punishment is forthcoming. Remember: forgiveness is not condoning or excusing an action; it is letting go of the negative emotions that can control our lives. In *How to Forgive – Even When You Can't Forget*, Thomas Herold reminds us that sometimes anger just feels good. "It inspires us and puts a fire in our belly. Soon, we live in that angry place because we cannot remember how it felt to be happy — anger may begin to feel more natural to us than happiness."[8]

How Do We Forgive? Where Do We Start?

If forgiving is the answer to finding peace, hope, gratitude, and joy in our lives, why don't we just do it? There are so many benefits to forgiveness; we wonder why it is so difficult in practice. Yet we all struggle with it. This question has an easy answer: forgiving someone is hard! Another reason is that we don't know how to do it properly. And then there's the underlying fear that by forgiving someone, we are inviting him or her to hurt us again or that we are condoning the person's offense.

Professionals working in the mental health field remind us that forgiveness should be a way of life, not a one-time action.

---

8   Thomas Herold, *How to Forgive Even When You Can't Forget* (Fairfax, CA: Dream Manifesto, 2009), 38.

The act of forgiving shouldn't be a rare event, but it should be something we do regularly; in fact, it needs to be practiced daily. We must learn that every time we remember how we've been hurt, we must release the hurt. When Jesus was asked how often we should forgive someone who sins against us, he said seventy times seven. In other words, we just keep forgiving. We can't go too long in our daily lives before we have an opportunity to forgive someone. We may not verbally lash out, but we get upset in our thoughts without even realizing we need to forgive. The best way to practice forgiveness is to immediately lift up the person who's offended us. "Don't let the sun go down on your wrath"(Eph. 4:26). Don't let the incident grow roots and take control of your heart.

The literature is replete with the "how to"of forgiveness. Let me share an example of the "Instructions" for forgiveness suggested by Sherri Carter in an article "How to Practice Forgiveness and Letting Go of the Anger." Give them a try; see if they work for you.

1. List the wrongs you feel have been done to you. For example, let's say someone betrayed your trust.
2. Look at each example one at a time. Ask yourself why you feel this was wrong. In our example of betrayed trust, you feel this was wrong because you trusted the person. This is setting you up for the next steps.
3. Next, think and write about how this situation made you feel. Besides being angry at the offender, look at how you feel about yourself. In our example, maybe you're angry because you knew you shouldn't have trusted that person, but you did anyway. Or maybe you feel foolish because you trusted him or her.

4. Determine why you have an emotional attachment to this event, why it matters to you what another person does, and what are you getting out of holding on to the anger/resentment/victim mode? Staying with our example, the emotional attachment to someone who betrayed your trust could result from wanting to be mad so *he or she is* not right. An emotional attachment doesn't have to make sense; in fact, it very rarely does.

5. Decide what the risk is to let the anger go. What would you be giving up? Letting go, for example, could mean you couldn't be mad anymore, and then what?

6. Realize that letting go of the anger is how to practice forgiveness. It doesn't make the other person right; it makes you free. You don't have to let another person determine who you are, whether by his or her actions or words. You don't have to be emotionally attached to another's opinion of you or anyone else's definition of you. You only have to determine who you are and stand in integrity with that. True forgiveness isn't about forgetting and turning the other cheek. In fact, it doesn't have anything at all to do with the other person. Only you.[9]

In my reading of the "how to" of forgiveness, I was reminded that forgiveness involves recognizing that the person who harmed us is more than just the agent of that harm. He or

---

9   Sherri Carter, "How to Practice Forgiveness and Letting go of the Anger," ehow.com, accessed January 27, 2011, http://www.ehow.com/how_5971189_practice-forgiveness-letting-go-anger.html.

she is, in fact, whether we want to acknowledge it or not, a human being whose full dimension isn't defined by the foolish decision to harm us in some way. Are we forgiving enough to recognize that, sometimes, good people do bad things and, sometimes, bad people turn good? At its core, forgiveness is an acknowledgment that a person who harmed us still has the capacity to be good. Also, we must recognize the fact that we can never build ourselves up by putting others down.

Forgiveness can be challenging. Forgiving someone can be particularly hard if the person doesn't admit to doing wrong or doesn't speak of his or her sorrow. Dr. Piderman, staff chaplain at the Mayo Clinic, suggests writing in a journal, praying, or using guided meditation.[10] "You may want to talk with someone you've found to be wise and compassionate, such as a spiritual leader, a mental health provider, or an unbiased family member or friend. You may also want to reflect on times you've hurt others and on those who have forgiven you. Keep in mind that forgiveness has the potential to increase your sense of integrity, peace, and overall well-being."[11]

The Link between Forgiveness and Health

Psychologist Loren Toussaint of Luther University in Iowa was among the first to demonstrate a long-term link between people's health and their ability to forgive.[12] In what many call the new science of forgiveness, overwhelming numbers of case studies cited in the *Harvard Health Publications* have shown the following physical and psychological benefits:

10   "Forgiveness: Letting Go," Mayo Clinic.

11   Ibid.

12   Lanphier, "Health Resolution."

- Reduced stress and hostility
- Fewer symptoms of depression
- Lower risk of alcohol and substance abuse
- Improved heart function or lower blood pressure
- Improved relationships
- Greater spiritual and psychological well-being
- Improved sleep.[13]

Dr. Loretta Lanphier writes that "The negative effects of prolonged anger and resentment have also been well documented, showing links to serious physical ailments, such as anxiety disorders, depression, heart attack, high blood pressure, digestive disorders, and irregular heartbeat. Even low levels of resentment and anger can lead to decreased cognitive function and problem-solving capacity. Anger induces the "fight or flight" response, causing hyper-arousal in the body to handle the crisis properly. "The culminating stress on the body," she concludes, "mimics amphetamine intake, which can raise blood pressure, increase heart rate, and depress the body's immune response in order to focus on the immediate threat."[14]

Another study, cited by Elizabeth Scott and published in the *Personality and Social Psychology Bulletin*, found that "Forgiveness not only restores positive thoughts and feelings toward the offending party, but its benefits also spill over to positive behaviors toward others outside of the relationship. Forgiveness is associated with more volunteering,

---

13 "Forgiveness: Letting Go," Mayo Clinic.

14 Ibid.

donating to charities, and the performing of other altruistic behaviors (and the converse is true of non-forgiveness)."[15]

The Significance of Forgiving

Forgiveness is good for your body, your relationships, and your place in the world. This statement should be reason enough to convince virtually everyone to do the work of letting go of anger and working on forgiveness. One secret to enjoying life to the fullest is being fully present in the moment, not thinking or worrying about what happened an hour ago, who offended you today, or how you can get even.

An anecdote I recently read paints a beautiful picture of forgiveness. Once a warrior went to a wise monk and asked him, "What is the difference between heaven and hell?" The monk looked at this warrior, who was very large and muscular, and had a savage look about him. The monk replied, "You ignorant brute. You are nothing but a savage. Why would I waste time with you, teaching you about heaven and hell?" When the monk said that, the warrior's blood began to boil, and he was filled with anger and hatred. Suddenly, he couldn't control his temper and started beating up the monk. After a few moments, the warrior realized what a heinous act he was committing and stopped. The monk smiled and said, "That fit of anger is hell." The warrior was ashamed about his violent act and begged the monk to forgive him. The monk smiled again and said,

---

15   Elizabeth Scott, "The Benefits of Forgiveness," About.com, last updated January 16, 2012, http://stress.about.com/od/relationships/a/forgiveness.htm.

"You're asking for forgiveness is heaven." Almost every day we have a choice between anger and resentment or forgiveness. We can choose to respond in kind, which creates more of a hell, or with forgiveness, which creates heaven in our own lives on earth.

In Ecclesiastes (8:15) we read, "Eat, drink, and be merry, for tomorrow we die." Another old saying tells us, "There is no time like the present." Both are appropriate in a discussion of when to let go of resentment and embrace forgiveness. None of us know what the future holds. We cannot know what we may lose by holding on to bitterness for one more day. Tomorrow may be too late. One more day may rob us of the opportunity to forgive.

Is your heart filled with hatred, anger, or revenge toward someone who has offended you? Do these feelings occupy all your waking thoughts? Are they making you physically ill? Are you angry at God for what happened? Are you consumed with ways of "getting back"? When we have been hurt, our instinct is to strike back. We want to make the person pay for what he or she did. But exacting revenge steps over the line into God's territory, as Paul warned: "Do not take revenge, my dear friends, but leave room for God's wrath, for it is written: 'it is mine to avenge; I will repay', says the Lord" (Rom. 12:19).

If we cannot take revenge, then we must forgive. God commands it. In his book *Landmines in the Path of the Believer*, Charles Stanley says "We are to forgive so that we may enjoy God's goodness without feeling the weight of anger burning deep within our hearts. Forgiveness does not mean we recant the fact that what happened to us was wrong. Instead, we roll our burdens onto the Lord and allow Him to carry them for us."[16] Neil Anderson wrote in *Twelve Steps to Forgiveness*, "Don't wait to forgive until you feel like forgiving; you will never get there."[17]

Exercises in Forgiveness

- Create a culture of forgiveness in your home. This usually begins with a gracious tongue. Parents should be quick and sincere to speak grace into every corner of family life. The language of graces and manners — "please," "thank you," "excuse me," and "I'm sorry" — should flavor the family conversation. Parents should not tolerate disrespect, shrillness, or cynicism. Responsible parenting recognizes that these weeds choke out the garden of grace.
- One of the first all-important steps in forgiveness is to answer these three questions: Who hurt you? What hurt you? And why did this action offend you as it did?
- Express yourself! When contemplating how to forgive someone, what may be helpful is to express your feelings to the other person. If the relationship is important to you and you would like to maintain it, it may be very useful for you to tell the other person, in nonthreatening

16   Charles Stanley, *Landmines in the Path of the Believer: Avoiding the Hidden Dangers* (Nashville, TN: Thomas Nelson, 2007), quoted in Jack Zavada, "How to Forgive," About.com, accessed January 21, 2013, http://christianity.about.com/od/topicaldevotions/a/How-To-Forgive.htm.

17   Neil Anderson, "Twelve Steps to Forgiveness," accessed January 21, 2013, https://m.facebook.com/note.php?note_id=463866673665142&_ft_=fbid. 463866673665142&_rdr.

language, how his actions affected you. This expression is all part of letting go!

- The next time someone rains on your parade, pick up a pen and start journaling. Researchers at the University of Miami found that when people wrote about the benefits they received from something negative someone had done to them, as opposed to writing about their feelings, they tended to forgive more easily. Looking at the bright side and trying to see the good in the bad can make you happier and less stressed.

- Remember, forgiveness is not condoning or excusing! Forgiveness does not minimize, justify, or excuse the wrong that was done. Also, it does not deny the harm that was done nor the feelings the injustice produced. Further, forgiveness doesn't mean putting yourself in a position to be harmed again.

- Whenever the incident resurfaces in your mind, practice a stress-reduction technique as you remind yourself of your ability and intention to release the past and move forward. Breathe deeply. Again. Slower. Focus your attention on something you are grateful for right now.

- Do not wait for an apology. It would be great if the people who wronged us would see the error of their ways and beg our forgiveness, but they probably won't. The people you have to forgive may not be worthy of your forgiveness, but neither are you worthy of harming yourself further by holding on to hurt feelings.

- What if your offender has died? You can still forgive him or her. Write out a forgiveness speech and then burn it as an act of letting go and releasing someone, even though he or she is no longer alive.
- To forgive, we must let go of our anger. If we continue to hold on to anger, it often leaks out against others who have committed no crime against us, since it colors all our experiences, often ruining our ability to feel joy in many other aspects of life.
- When was the last time you reminded yourself that you cannot ever build yourself up by putting someone else down?

CHAPTER 4

Nature & the World around Us

God writes the gospel not in the Bible alone, but on trees and flowers and clouds and stars.

— MARTIN LUTHER

Nature...What Is It?

Nature is everything that is not man=made. So this definition excludes all things mankind introduced. All those human developments are summarized as culture. The definition of nature includes all natural objects, such as stones, animals, plants, the sun, smells, water, and snow. It also includes natural events, such as rain, earthquakes, fire, tornadoes, and thunderstorms. It refers to the physical world — the erosion of rocks, the turning of leaves, butterfly wings fluttering, coyotes singing, snow melting, waterfalls crashing, glaciers grinding, geese honking, and the list goes on.

Unfortunately, in the last hundred years there has been an extraordinary shift away from spending time experiencing these natural phenomena. This is mostly due to the enormous transition of our lives away from the rural areas and into cities. Never before in history have humans spent so little time in physical contact with animals, plants, and the dynamics of our natural environment. The consequences of this change are relatively unknown. Some research has already shown that too much artificial stimulation and existence spent in purely human environments may exacerbate exhaustion and result in a loss of vitality and health.

Natural Environments, Special Places

A new branch of psychotherapy, ecopsychology, is involved with healing the human/nature relationship. It's a sort of green psychotherapy. This new field assumes that when people feel disconnected from nature, this discord creates both human and environmental suffering. Linda Buzzell, speaking about her recently published book, *Ecotherapy: Healing with Nature in Mind*, tells us that the nature connection is "an unbelievably powerful healing methodology." She specifically points to a study completed at the University of Essex in the UK that found that connecting with nature through just a simple walk in natural surroundings was as powerful an antidepressant as an antidepressant medication in cases of mild to moderate depression. She explains, "The same way that we're embedded in a family or in community, we're embedded in the vastness of nature."[18]

If this is true, we need to ask ourselves if we should establish practices in our lives that make this connection. Too often our connections are with the cell phone, computer, television, or time on the sofa or at our desks. Have we established relationships in natural environments? Have these relationships become an important part of our lives? When we have highly valued experiences in specific places or settings, these places and settings assume particular importance for us and become special to us. People become attached to such places in the same way that they become attached to a good friend or family member.

To better understand the values and experiences that lead people to consider certain outdoor places as special, Herbert Schroeder carried out a series of open-ended, qualitative surveys, in which people wrote about special places and explained what these places meant to them. They were instructed to briefly describe each place and express whatever thoughts, feelings, memories, and associations came to mind in connection with these places.[19]

---

18 Linda Buzzell, "Ecotherapy: Slowing Down to Nature's Pace," *The Blog, Huffington Post*, June 9, 2009, http://www.huffingtonpost.com/linda-buzzell/ecotherapy-slowing-down-t_b_213288.html.

19 Herbert Schroeder, "Experiencing Nature in Special Places: Surveys in the North-Central Region," *Journal of Forestry*, 100 (July−August 2002): 8−14.

Beauty Is in the Eye of the Beholder

The characteristics of these special places are not the focus of this work. Rather, it is how we see and feel these natural places. How do they affect our souls? How do they revive our lives? Do they make our lives more significant? What is it about these places that draw us back for more? Schroeder's survey indicated a wide range of meanings, values, experiences, and memories associated with these special places. Many places were valued for their naturalness. The variety and diversity of animals, plants, and other natural features contributed to their appeal. Respondents appeared to enjoy observing natural processes and cycles of change such as the seasons and the weather of their special place.

Beauty was one of the most often-mentioned qualities of special places. It was often described in terms of the scenic features of the landscape. In addition, other senses, such as smell and hearing, often added to the aesthetic pleasure of special places. "For many respondents," Schroeder describes, "the experience of beauty went beyond pretty scenery to involve a deeper emotional response to the aesthetic character of the setting." Other respondents characterized their special places as awe inspiring, evoking a sense of wonder and magic.

Another frequently mentioned quality was quietness or serenity. The tranquility of the setting enabled respondents to relax and experience a sense of peacefulness within themselves. It provided an opportunity for meditation and reflection, and respondents reported feeling refreshed or renewed after visiting the place. Others experienced a sense of remoteness or isolation, which provided a feeling of being far away from the civilized world and escaping the stress of city life.

Anne Frank describes just how comforting nature can be: "The best remedy for those who are afraid, lonely or unhappy is to go outside; somewhere they can be quiet, alone with the heavens, nature and God. Because only then does one feel that all is as it should be and that God wishes to see people happy, amidst the simple beauty of nature. As long as this exists, and it certainly always will, I know that then there will always be comfort for every sorrow, whatever the circumstances may be. And I firmly believe that nature brings solace in all troubles."[20] Chuck Gallozzi characterizes nature as a "kind teacher."[21] Through the birds, it teaches us how to sing and compose music. Through the swaying reeds and fluttering butterflies, it teaches us how to dance. The majesty of the landscape and creatures teaches us art. The beauty and vastness of the universe teach us to wonder. Through a crack of thunder and a flash of day in a storming night, nature teaches us about fire. Squalls teach us how to be brave, and blizzards how to cope. Nature teaches us that the world is not about rewards or punishments but about consequences — that what we sow, we reap.

20　Anne Frank, *The Diary of a Young Girl: The Definitive Edition* (New York: Doubleday, 1995), quoted in Chuck Gallozzi, "Experiencing Nature," personal-development.com, April 20, 2009, http://www. personal-development.com/chuck/nature.htm.

21　Chuck Gallozzi, "Experiencing Nature," personal-development. com, April 20, 2009, http://www.personal-development.com/chuck/ nature.htm.

Significance of Nature

The term *ecopsychology*, first coined by writer and theorist Theodore Roszak in his 1992 book, *Voice of the Earth*, is loosely defined as the connection between ecology and human psychology. "Roszak argues that humans can heal what he calls their 'psychological alienation' from nature and build a more sustainable society if they recognize we all have an innate bond with the natural world. Roszak's basic premise is that we operate under the illusion that we people are separate from nature but that, on the contrary, humans are more apt to derive comfort and even inspiration from the natural world than from the relatively recent construct of modern urban society. Distancing ourselves from nature, Roszak maintains, has negative psychological consequences and also leads to ecological devastation at the hands of society that, as a result, lacks empathy for nature."[22]

While many psychotherapists have adopted aspects of ecopsychology in treating various mental illnesses and psychological disorders, the teachings of Roszak and others in the still-evolving field can be helpful even for those not in need of a therapist's care. John V. Davis, a university professor who teaches and writes about ecopsychology, says that "meditating in the outdoors, participating in wilderness retreats, and becoming involved in nature-based festivals or celebrations of the season…have been shown to have healing effects in the elderly and in people with psychological disabilities." He also concludes that "join-

---

22   Roddy Scheer and Doug Moss, "Earth Talk - Questions & Answers About Our Environment," *The Environmental Magazine*, November 1, 2008, http://www.emagazine.com/view/4443.

ing in earth-nurturing activities, such as environmental restoration or advocacy work, and spending time around animals, including pets, have also been found to benefit the psychological health of ordinary people in their everyday lives."[23]

Getting children involved with nature and the outdoors is viewed by eco-psychology advocates as a key to their development, especially in the present technological age. Richard Louv, author of *Last Child in the Woods: Saving Our Children from Nature-Deficit Disorder*, argues that children are so plugged into television and video games that they've lost their connection to the natural world. This disconnect, Louv maintains, has led not only to poor physical fitness among our youth (including obesity) but also to long-term mental and spiritual health problems.[24]

A growing body of scientific evidence has identified a strong correlation between experience in the natural world and children's ability to learn, along with their physical and emotional health. Time spent in nature also positively affects stress levels, attention-deficit hyperactivity disorder, and cognitive functioning. Researchers at Indiana University School of Medicine, Purdue University, and the University of Washington reported that greener neighborhoods are associated with slower increases in children's body mass, no matter how congested the neighborhood is.[25]

---

23 Gallozzi, "Experiencing Nature."

24 Richard Louv, *Last Child in the Woods: Saving Our Children from Nature-Deficit Disorder* (Chapel Hill, NC: Algonquin Books, 2008),

25 Richard Louv, "A Walk in the Woods," *Orion*, March/April 2009, http://www.orionmagazine.org/index.php/articles/article/4401/.

In 2001, Frances Kuo and colleagues at the University of Illinois at Urbana-Champaign published a study examining the relationship between levels of vegetation and crime rates in ninety-eight apartment buildings in a Chicago public housing development. Compared with housing blocks that had little or no vegetation, those with high levels of greenery had 48 percent fewer property crimes and 56 percent fewer violent crimes.[26]

Research from the Netherlands and Japan has revealed that people living close to natural surroundings live longer and enjoy a better and healthier life. A Swedish study concluded that if office personnel could view greenery through their office windows, their stress levels during working hours were significantly reduced.[27] There is a new theory that being grounded (barefoot in contact with the earth or water) has an energizing effect on the body. Shoes insulate us from the earth. By grounding or "earthing," we are connected to the earth's energy. When we sit on the grass, walk barefoot on the beach, or swim in the ocean, we all feel great.

Connecting to Nature

Where do you find your own time? Think about this question: where do you go to get away from it all? Do you have a special place? How do you free yourself from that frazzled feeling, from being out of sync with your deepest self? Do

---

26 Sue Cartlege, "Mental Health Benefits from Nature," suite101. com,May21,2008,http://suite101.com/article/mental-health-benefits-from-nature-a54608.

27 Cecily Maller, et al., "Healthy Nature Healthy People: 'Contact with Nature' as an Upstream Health Promotion Intervention for Populations." *Health Promotion International*, 21, no. 1 (2006): 45−54.

you go beyond noticing the gorgeous, deep, velvety reds of the Japanese maple tree or the clearness of the blue sky in autumn that provides a backdrop to the clouds in a usually overcast sky?

Too often, although we may notice the special effects of nature, including their beauty and even their perfection, we fail to go that extra step and really connect with nature: feeling the trees and their dance of interconnectedness, feeling as if we ourselves are bursting into bloom with the geraniums in the pot on the patio, or becoming the hummingbird intent on gorging nectar to gather energy to combat the cold winds of the coming winter. By denying a true connection with nature, we deny an essential aspect of ourselves.

Linda Buzzell refers to the research that confirms the "nature connection" and its potential as a healing methodology. She discusses the concept of "time poverty" as a recognized psychological and social stressor. In our highly complex society, there just isn't enough time for everything: our demanding jobs, our bureaucratic responsibilities, our loved ones, to mention a few. In this constant rush, we inevitably fall further behind in our connections with nature.

In *The Ransomed Heart,* John Eldredge writes,

Nature is not primarily functional. It is primarily beautiful. Stop for a moment and let that sink in. We're so used to evaluating everything (and everyone) by their usefulness, this thought will take a minute or two to dawn on us. Nature is not primarily functional. It is primarily *beautiful*. Which is to say, beauty is in and of itself a great and glorious good, something we need in large and daily doses (for our God has seen fit to arrange for this). Nature at the height of its glory shouts, *Beauty is essential*! Revealing that Beauty is the essence of God. The whole world is full of his glory.[28]

A Special Story

Not only am I an only child, but I come from a very small family. I grew up with my parents, my mother's parents, and her sister, Aunt Mary, more affectionately called Mar. As the only child in the family, I was the apple of everyone's eye, especially Mar. We spent much time together, and most of that time was out of doors. Whether bathing our feet in the upper Niagara River, fishing, walking the Niagara Gorge, feeding the ducks at Hyde Park, or just sitting by Bond's Lake, I'm sure my appreciation for nature has evolved from those excursions. Mar is still with us but unfortunately is now in the throes of dementia. A few weeks ago I was rummaging through her memorabilia and found this handwritten story titled "A Surprise."

> One summer day I was driving along looking for a lawn bursting with sunny dandelion blooms.
>
> Seeing so much spiritualism in the dandelion, I wanted to find an especially beautiful one to press in plastic for my Bible. So I began my venture.

---

28 John Eldredge, *The Ransomed Heart: A Collection of Devotional Readings* (Nashville: Thomas Nelson, 2005), 45.

I spotted a rather large patch close to the road and stopped. Delightedly I began my search from blossom to blossom finding it difficult to make a choice: There was something uniquely lovely in all that met my gaze. At last, looking down directly in front of me, a bee nestled deep in the center of a dandelion caught my attention, and without further thought I decided that what was good enough for a bee would be good enough for me. I reached down to pick it and to my surprise, there was not only one bee replenishing its supply of nectar, but two!

While holding it in my hand, I laughed out loud, oblivious to my surroundings, and still standing motionless began to wonder with the wonderment of a child at what I had seen. In all my study of nature, never had I been made aware of bees finding any sweetness in dandelions. What began as a delightful surprise ended in an unforgettable lesson in humility. But if I had not moved my muscles to stoop, I would have missed the reward.

Exercises in Nature

- Walk slowly and breathe in your surroundings.
- Clear your mind of all clutter and worries accumulated through daily living. This cleansing process can occur naturally during an extended stay in the wilderness.
- Break the habit of looking at the same things over and over again. Instead, force your eyes to look at new

things. Or look at familiar things with the eyes of a child as if you hadn't seen them before.

- Open your ears. Turn up the volume of everything around you. Can you hear the road? The wind? Learn to pick out sounds within sounds.
- Get down on all fours and notice the smells around you.
- Spend just five minutes doing something in a park, in the woods, or even in your backyard, sitting quietly and soaking up the smells, sights, and feelings of the setting.
- Reconnect with plants. A simple pot on a windowsill slows us down to the pace of a seed, a seedling, a leaf, or a flower.
- Spend more time outdoors in wild nature. Most of us are indoors most of the time. Our bodies and souls cry out for long walks on a beach, contemplation in a forest, or a few minutes sitting by a waterfall or a rambling brook. These times slow life down to a healing natural pace.
- If you have never experienced a sunrise or sunset, then make it a point to do so soon. Observing nature's wonder is the first step in the healing process the sun provides.
- Hang pictures of nature scenes in your work space, especially if you have no natural views. They will help you feel God's creative power.

CHAPTER 5

Relationships

A friend might be reckoned the masterpiece of nature.

— RALPH WALDO EMERSON

Relationships and You

When our lives come to an end, how successful we've been or how many assets we've accumulated won't really matter. What will be important is that we have built meaningful relationships. In fact, a life is wasted if it has not had an impact on the lives of others. Investing our time and effort in people is rewarding and meaningful to our lives.

Someone once said that no man (or woman) is an island. And that's true. Some people will make your heart sing. There are people who will bring you closer to God. There are people who will make you laugh, and there are people who will make you cry. Relationships are all about being with someone who likes you, who thinks you're someone special.

Unfortunately, our society appears to be experiencing a diminishing desire to engage in personal relationships. We Americans have one-third as many close friends and confidants as we did just two decades ago — a sign that we may be living lonelier, more isolated, lives than we did in the past. In 1985, the average American had three people in whom he or she could confide matters that were important to him or her, says a study in the *American Sociological Review* conducted by Professor Lynn Smith-Lovin. By 2004, that number had dropped to two people, and one in four had no close confidants at all.[29]

The Partnership Advantage suggests that national statistics reflect a growing distrust and division in our relationships. Consider the following:

- The divorce rate is 45 percent and growing.
- Hate crimes are near ten thousand annually.
- About 33 percent of women report domestic abuse.

---

29 Janet Kornblum, "Study: 25% of Americans Have No One to Confide in," *USA Today*, June 22, 2006, http://www.usatoday.com/news/nation/2006-06-22-friendship_x.htm.

- Child abuse cases now number more than eight hundred thousand per year.
- Annual gun-related casualties have reached one hundred thousand.
- Mental problems have been found in 26 percent of Americans.

Joanne Black, Senior Vice-President of Marketing with The Partnership Advantage, comments, "We all hunger for moments of spontaneous interaction, authentic intimacy and unquestioned love; that connectedness that makes us feel whole. We hunger because these experiences are too few and far between in our relationships…all of them…at home, at work, in the community and around the world."[30]

Building relationships is part of every individual's life and is helpful in the enrichment of one's life. Close friends are a refuge from the negative experiences of life. They lend a helping hand in times of trouble, a shoulder to lean on, and a smile to brighten up life. Peer relationships help enhance one's interpersonal skills and leadership qualities in childhood, help one fight his or her problems, help express oneself in adolescence, and help overcome solitude in later life. Relationships with peers in the workplace help enrich one's professional life. They enhance the positive atmosphere at work, increasing satisfaction and productivity. Peer relationships play a part in every walk of life.

Every day you may mix with other people. You might hang out with them because you want to or because you

---

30 "Personal Relationships," The Partnership Advantage, http:// www.partnershipadvantage.net/personal.html, accessed March 1, 2011, http://www.partnershipadvantage.net/personal.html.

have no choice. You might really like them, or you might not think much of them at all. Relationships are not just about who you are "going with" or "getting it on with." They are about all the interactions you have with people every day.

Here are some examples of the major categories of relationships we experience:

- Family—you may or may not live with them, you may get along with them or have frequent fights, you may never have met them, or they may be your best friends.
- Peers—some might be your closest mates; others might be people you don't like at all.
- People at school or work—you might not hang out with them were it not for school or work.
- Your love partner—he or she could be your best mate or the person who irritates you most.
- Your neighbor—you might meet regularly or never meet; all of us have a relationship with our common community, whether we feel like we are part of it or separate from it.

Family Relationships Are Where Relationships Begin

Uncovering the importance of family isn't difficult. You may or may not be aware of it, but your family was the first school you entered. When you came into this world, you were unfit to survive on your own. However, your arrival made your family happy, and they took you home. Then, from day one, you started learning about love, care, and family relationships.

Your family defines who you are as a person. Family enables us to feel a sense of belonging and who we are. It's a source of comfort and support, warmth, security, and protection; and it helps us to make sense of the world in which we live. Within the family you can be yourself and be admitted for who you are. There are no terms or conditions for membership.

Your family supports you when troubles surround you. It helps you endure through good times and bad; it brings happiness and pleasure to your life. "Within the family unit," says John Rowlinson, "each member has their own individual aspirations in addition to being part of the collective unit. Each member should be made to feel unique and special and encouraged to follow their goals and dreams." But it's not like *The Waltons*, the article continues. "It's understandable that families quarrel and experience conflict sometimes. The important aspect is that each member should feel that they can express their opinions openly and that their voice is as important as any other family member's. Conflicts and rows and how a healthy family resolves their differences are one of the most important elements of family life, as it sets up the younger members to gain an understanding of how they might deal with conflict when they become adults."[31]

Today, most of us are so busy, constantly in motion, that maintaining close relationships—even with our spouses and immediate families—proves challenging. We work long hours to provide for the people we love, to give them luxuries and benefits we may not have experienced ourselves,

---

31   John Rowlinson, "About Our Site," Life Coach Expert, November 29, 2010, http://www.lifecoachexpert.co.uk/aboutoursite.html.

but we miss spending quality time with them. We can give them expensive gifts and vacations, but we struggle to give them our time and individual attention. In *One Month to Live*, Kerry and Chris Shook ask provocative questions: "So why don't we live as if our relationships matter most? Why do we wait until people are dead to give them flowers?"[32] Ironically, most of us value relationships highly but don't put forth the energy to invest in them fully. In the hyper-speed hustle of our overscheduled lives, many of us tend to take others for granted. A spouse can become just another supporting player, a roommate who helps with the finances. Our children turn into people who burden our schedules when they need us to take them to school, soccer practice, or the mall. Family get-togethers become social obligations, like the company Christmas party. But if we had only one month to live, we would suddenly realize we need other people as much as they need us.

What you learned from your family became your value system; it forms the way you perceive things and act. An individual is known by his or her actions. Your family gave you an identity — a value system. These values are the guidelines or rudders of our lives, and they help us decide what is right and wrong. Families can mean totally different things to different people.

In his 2000 book, *Bowling Alone*, Robert Putnam suggests that people are finding fewer relationships in clubs and neighbors; they are relying more on family. The percentage of people who confide only in family members has increased from 57 percent to 80 percent in the past several years, and

---

32 Shook and Shook, *One Month to Live*, 66.

the number of those who depend totally on a spouse is up from 5 percent to 9 percent.[33]

Take time now to reflect on the meaning of your family relationships with your mother, father, siblings, and other relatives. How has their presence or absence affected your life? What has family meant to you? Is your family a significant aspect of your life?

Friends and Your Social Well-Being

Making friends is something that might seem to come easily for some and be very hard for others. No matter what you've done in the past or how many friends you may already have, making new friends is always a good idea. Anaïs Nin suggested that "each friend represents a world within us, a world possibly not born until they arrive, and it is only by this meeting that a new world is born."[34] Though some natural loners are happy without friends, most of us depend greatly on the company of true friends.

When we consider friendships, we usually think in terms of two people. However, Tom Rath and James Harter, authors of *Your Friends and Your Social Wellbeing,* suggest that our entire social network affects our health, habits, and well-being; and mutual friendships matter even more. These are relationships in which we and one of our close friends share a friendship with a third person. Investing in

---

33 Robert Putnam, *Bowling Alone: The Collapse and Revival of American Community* (New York: Simon and Schuster, 2000).

34 Anaïs Nin *The Diary of Anaïs Nin, Vol. 1, 1931 – 1934,* ed. Gunther Stuhlmann (New York: Houghton Mifflin Harcourt, 1969), quoted in "All About Friendship," *Psychology Today,* accessed January 21, 2013, http://www.psychologytoday.com/basics/friends.

these mutual relationships will lead to even higher levels of well-being. This is why doing what we can to strengthen the entire social network around us is critical for us.[35]

Results generated from this study also suggest that the sheer amount of time we spend socializing matters. The data suggest that to thrive we need six hours of daily social time. When we get at least six hours, our well-being increases, and stress and worry lessen. It is important to note that the six hours include time at work, at home, on the telephone talking to friends, through e-mails, on Facebook and Twitter, and through other forms of communication.

Beyond the immediate increase in well-being that comes with each hour of social time, the long-term benefits can be even more profound, particularly as we age. A study of more than fifteen thousand people over the age of fifty found that among those who were socially active, their memories declined at less than half the rate of those who were least social.

Living in an Intimate Relationship

Some of us search our entire lives for a feeling of oneness with another person — the opportunity to share not just the burdens of life but its pleasures too as well as our strengths and beauty. We want the powerful impact of our internal experiences to make an impression on someone else, as if to say that we count, we are whole, and we want to impart this feeling to another person. We long to be rid of that

---

35 Tom Rath and James K. Harter, "Your Friends and Your Social Wellbeing," *Gallup Business Journal*, accessed on January 21, 2013, http:// gmj.gallup.com/content/127043/friends-social-wellbeing.aspx.

dark feeling of being alone. Catie Conklin Trafford, a family therapist, concludes that our intimate experiences may involve our emotional, cognitive, social, physical, sexual, and spiritual lives. Two people, each of whom is in touch with his or her own internal experiences, may be able to share an intimate relationship on any one of these levels.[36]

Wikipedia defines "intimate relationship" as "a particularly close interpersonal relationship...characterized as an enduring behavioral interdependence, repeated interactions, emotional attachment and need fulfillment." Intimacy generally refers to a very close, affective connection with another person, resulting from a bond formed through knowledge and experience of the other person. Love is usually an aspect of this type of interaction and includes physical and emotional intimacy. Although these relationships are only a small subset of interpersonal relationships, they are among our most significant.

The capacity for love gives depth to human relationships, brings people closer to each other physically and emotionally, and makes people think expansively about themselves and their place in this world. In his triangular theory of love, psychologist Robert Sternberg theorizes that love is a mix of three components: (1) passion or physical attraction, (2) intimacy or feelings of closeness, and (3) commitment involving the decision to initiate and sustain a relationship. The presence of all three components characterizes consummate love, the most durable type of love. Positive conse-

---

36 Catie Conklin-Trafford, "The Intimate Relationship," *Emotional Wellness Matters,* 12, no. 5, accessed January 24, 2013, http://www.successfultherapymatters.com/newsletters.html.

quences of being in love include increased self-esteem and self- efficacy.[37]

Each person seems to understand intimate experiences in his or her own way. In a sense learning how to share intimacy with another person takes a journey of personal discovery. Where are you on this journey?

Without a Friend, Work Is a Lonely Place

Gallup has conducted extensive studies on the value of the workplace. One of the most revealing questions asked of more than fifteen million employees all over the world is whether they have a "best friend at work." The key to this question is "best friend." The research revealed that just 30 percent had a best friend at work. Those who did are seven times more likely to be engaged in their jobs, are better at engaging customers, produce higher-quality work, have a higher sense of well-being, and are less likely to get injured on the job.

What is it about a close relationship in the workplace that makes such a profound difference? To find out, Gallup researchers examined moment-by-moment experiences throughout the course of the day that lead to higher well-being and work engagement. The study revealed that the single-best predictor of higher well-being is not *what* people are doing but *who* they are doing it with. It also determined that employees value their jobs more when they enjoy good friendships at the workplace. One of the greatest deterrents to productivity is feeling ostracized or alienated by coworkers. Colleagues who are friends are more likely to support

---

37 "Interpersonal Relationships," Wikipedia, accessed March 1, 2011, http://en.wikipedia.org/wiki/Interpersonal_relationship.

one another when presented with challenges or new responsibilities; this support enhances workflow and team spirit.[38]

According to a study conducted by a team of MIT researchers, in which workers wore high-tech identity badges throughout the day that monitored their movements and conversations, found that idle chitchat might actually be valuable to productivity. The research found that even small increases in social cohesiveness led to large gains in productivity.[39]

The Significance of Relationships

Professional health-care workers at the Mayo Clinic have concluded that friendship connections can:

- Increase your sense of belonging and purpose in life.
- Boost your happiness.
- Reduce stress.
- Improve your sense of self-worth.
- Decrease your risk of serious mental illness.
- Help you weather personal traumas, such as divorce, serious illness, job loss, or the death of a loved one.
- Encourage you to change unhealthy lifestyles or habits, such as excessive drinking or lack of exercise.
- Share in your good times, such as a new baby, job, or house.[40]

---

38 Rath and Harter, "Your Friends."

39 Ibid.

40 "Friendships: Enrich Your Life and Improve Your Health," Mayo Clinic, accessed April 16, 2011, http://www.mayoclinic.com/health/friendships/MH00125.

Relationships serve as a buffer during tough times, which in turn improves cardiovascular functioning and decreases stress levels. On the other hand, people with very few social ties have nearly twice the risk of dying from heart disease and are twice as likely to catch colds, even though they are less likely to be exposed to germs that come from frequent social contact. Another study revealed that wounds took twice as long to heal for couples who reported hostility in their relationships. So a strained relationship could extend the time it takes to recover from surgery or a major injury.

In another series of studies, researchers found that socially isolated people are two to five times more likely to die prematurely than those who have a sense of connection and community. Women with metastatic breast cancer were assigned to a support group that met once a week for a year. Women in the support group lived twice as long as those not in such groups.[41]

A study at the University of Texas looked at patients who had undergone open-heart surgery. Those who neither participated in a group nor derived strength from their religion were more than seven times as likely to die by six months after their surgery.[42]

Statistics tell us that married people live longer than singles. A new medical study suggests that marriage also wards off the debilitating memory loss that often occurs in the aging process. People who were widowed or divorced at midlife and remained so are at greater risk of developing Alzheimer's disease. Being single at midlife is also a risk factor. The "marriage effect" lowers these risks. Reporting

---

41   Conklin-Trafford, "The Intimate Relationship."

42   Ibid.

in the *British Medical Journal*, Dr. Ranit Mishori indicates that the marriage effect appears to be influenced not by how much education the individuals have attained, how much physical exercise they get, or whether they otherwise had active social lives — all factors other studies have found to be important in determining the risk of dementia.[43]

Joie Schmidt summarizes the pricelessness of relationships well:

A true friend reminds you of everything that lies within your heart. They act as a mirror when you have sometimes lost sight and forgotten who you really are, what you believe in, etc. They pick you up when you forget that you can do so on your own. They remind you that people do not hurt others purposely, but that they can only treat others as good as they treat themselves. They remind you that tomorrow will hold infinite doors to limitless possibilities giving you the energy and belief in yourself to continue to walk through any and all doors that you want to walk through.[44]

Remembering to give thanks on a daily basis for all our genuine friendships in our lives is important. This includes

---

43   Hadley Finch, "Your Guide to Healthy Relationships: How Do Singles Get the Health Benefits of the Marriage Effect," ezinearticles.com, http://ezinearticles.com/?Your-Guide-to-Healthy-Relationships---How-Do-Singles-Get-the-Health-Benefits-of-the-Marriage-Effect?&id=2813388.

44   Joie Schmidt, "It is Priceless, It is a Treasure, It is a Gift," socyberty.com, April 7, 2007, http://socyberty.com/people/the - value-of-true-friendship/2/.

all those who did not have our best interest in life, for they have probably taught us how to love ourselves more, realizing the true value of our worth.

For all the benefits we derive from living in a highly technological world, we may still find it difficult to discover ways to form intimate relationships. In fact, our high-tech society seems to fragment our social connections and drive us away from other people. For example, e-mail seems to make connecting with other people much easier, but in truth our messages are usually just flashes of ideas—briefly written, briefly read, and instantaneously deleted. They barely satisfy our desire for more complete relationships based on our inner experiences. As technological devices distract us even more, we need to guard against advances that detract from our previous ways of seeing, hearing, or touching other people.

Linda Ellis says it best: "Remember that our true worth and significance comes not from what we have accomplished or attained, but in the legacy we have left in the hearts and minds of those we've loved and who have loved us. When all is said and done, what will matter most are those relationships and bonds we've created through time with the people in our lives with whom we've shared love, laughter and memories."[45]

Exercises in Relationships

- Join or start a group. Examples of such groups are book clubs, Bible study groups, church groups, workout groups, hobby clubs, mothers-night-out

---

45   Linda Ellis, "The Dash," Retrieved from http://lindaellis.net/the-dash-poem-by-linda-ellis/.

groups, and men's groups. Participation in this type of activity allows you to make and maintain new friendships. Seeing someone once every few weeks is sufficient to keep a friendship alive, so meeting in a group setting is efficient because you can see many people at once — you're creating a social network.

- Do lunch. Invite an acquaintance to join you for breakfast, lunch, or dinner.

- Volunteer. Hospitals, places of worship, museums, and community centers often need volunteers. You can form strong connections when you work with people who share a mutual interest.

- Do you listen? Listening — truly listening — can reduce conflict, boost trust, and lead to a more satisfying relationship. Listening may sound simple, but it requires more than being in the same room where the person is speaking. Signal that you care by turning off the television, offering your undivided attention, and making eye contact.

- Learn to give and accept praise. Compliment people on their character, not on their appearance. If you don't accept praise, people will eventually stop giving it.

- Avoid "winning" situations. If you "win" a discussion, it is at the expense of someone else, and you will have to deal with that person's feelings. No one is right all the time, nor can you be all things to all people all of the time.

- Let them know you care. Remember people's birthdays, anniversaries, likes and dislikes, and any other particulars about them. Let them know you care about them by sending a note of gratitude, making a short phone call, or offering assistance.

- Be constructive. Let people know you value their friendship. People are drawn to other people who share their root beliefs. Inject cheerfulness into your relationships. Don't cast a negative shadow; chase the clouds away; be uplifting and positive.
- Forgiveness is essential in friendships. Accepting friends, even though they may make a mistake, shows them that you respect them enough to see past their human errors.
- Treat coworkers with respect. Regardless of whether you develop friendships with all your coworkers, you should treat everyone respectfully. While you definitely shouldn't allow anyone to take advantage of your good nature, you should make an effort to be friendly and polite to all your coworkers. These actions demonstrate the depth of your character.

CHAPTER 6

Generosity

You make a living by what you get.
You make a life by what you give.

— WINSTON CHURCHILL

Generosity: Only for the Rich?

Too often we think generosity is reserved for people who are either very rich or very holy. We know being selfish is completely unacceptable, but we reserve generosity for another day—like when we win the lottery or make it really big. Sure, we were taught at an early age that sharing, kindness, and fairness are all values to be embraced and practiced. But genuine and even lavish generosity is something for the rich and famous.

While reading *Radical* by David Platt, I was challenged to think of my own "richness." I usually don't think of myself as being rich, but, as Platt reminds readers, "if you and I have running water, shelter over your heads, clothes to wear, food to eat and some means of transportation (even if it is public transportation), then we are in the top 15 percent of the world's people of wealth." His word picture humbled me: "Every Sunday we gather in a multi-million dollar building with millions of dollars in vehicles parked outside. We leave worship to spend thousands of dollars on lunch before returning to our hundreds of millions of dollars' worth of homes. We live in luxury. Meanwhile, the poor man stands outside our gate."[46]

How Are We Generous?

People are generous in all kinds of ways. They give loose change to beggars on street corners, contribute their money to charities, volunteer their time in hospitals, and donate food and supplies to earthquake victims. We give materially in terms of goods and money. We give time and service. We give care. In some situations one could say that giving a person space is a kind of generosity; just allowing someone to be the way he or she is, is a type of giving. As leaders, we

---

46   David Platt, *Radical: Taking Back Your Faith from the American Dream* (Colorado Springs, CO: Multnomah, 2010), 114–115.

allow room for employees' initiatives, even for bad choices and errors. As parents and teachers, we can free the young from overly restrictive rules and not demand that they see everything as we do. In the marriage oath the commands to "love and respect" and "become one flesh" are generous acts.

Life is exciting, but that doesn't mean it isn't stressful. We're bound to run into difficulties and sure to get caught in the storms of life. When we do, we appreciate the extended hand of a friend offering help. Whatever form generosity may take, it is like the sun breaking through a bank of black clouds to the person who receives it.

We can see from these examples that these acts of giving and generosity can be quite varied. Varied as they may be, it is through them that we develop a "spirit" of generosity. This spirit requires us to see beyond ourselves and to reflect on our passion to help others.

Motives for Generosity

It is not the intent of this work to review the efforts of those who have sought the reasons why people are generous. It is, however, worth being reminded that the world's cultures and great religions have long sought to answer the question of how we should live; and they have often responded that it has to do with how we treat others, particularly those most in need. Ample evidence lies at the heart of what it means to be thoughtful and moral human beings.

The apostle Paul reminds us in 1 Timothy that we were created to give; we were created to be generous. Jesus said it is more blessed to give than to receive (Acts 20:35). And Proverbs 11:25 tells us, "A generous man will prosper, he who refreshes others will himself be refreshed." The word for *prosper* literally means "fat"; so the sentence implies that generous people will be obese but overflowing with abundance.

While we are tempted to think that the things we own and the money we have are ours, those possessions are ultimately God's. Believing that everything we have belongs to God can be a struggle. We think that because we have worked so hard for it, we earned it, and it is rightly ours. We must always remember that we brought nothing into this world, and we will take nothing out of it.

The tradition of helping others is well recorded in antiquity. For example, the following verses reveal that helping the poor was a custom thirty-three hundred years ago. "When you reap the harvest of your land, you shall not reap your fields to its very border, neither shall you gather the gleanings after your harvest. And you shall not strip your vineyards bare, neither shall you gather the fallen grapes of your vineyard; you shall leave them for the poor and for the sojourner" (Lev. 19:9–10). Again, in Isaiah 58:10–11, it is written, "Feed the hungry! Help those in trouble."

That every great religion places such strong emphasis on the virtue of generosity is no accident. Generosity not only enables society to work more effectively but also has a profound spiritual effect on both giver and receiver. In helping our neighbors, we also serve our own inner beings.

Have you ever thought about the fact that Scripture never really records Jesus giving money to anyone? Yet when you think of generous living, Jesus leads the way. Why do you think that is? Could it be because Jesus knew that giving is not just about money but is an action of the heart?

There's plenty of evidence to prove the value of generosity even aside from the Bible. Simple observation clearly shows that people who behave in a miserly, greedy, selfish way are miserable. There's a reason Ebenezer Scrooge is no one's role model.

Too often in our effort to accumulate the things of life, we forget that a willingness to be generous can be a great source of happiness. There is a real joy in being generous. It warms our hearts to do an act of kindness or to go even further than that and give away some of the wealth we have accumulated. One of the greatest dangers of the accumulation of wealth is the effect it has upon our character. A continuous temptation is to forgo all the natural feelings of generosity and live for the mere purpose of accumulating the things of our world. At this point we ask if this accumulation is the real meaning of living. Is this all there is? Growing up in a capitalistic society, most of us have gleaned that what we own is more important that what we have to offer. But generosity is what truly defines us and shows others who we are. It gives significance to our lives.

The older we get, the more we realize that the things we spent most of our lives thinking were the most important suddenly seem unimportant. In the end, does it matter how high we climbed the corporate ladder, often sacrificing time with family and friends? In the end, does it matter that we bought all that stuff that now clutters our attics, basements, and garages? It can be painful to look back and realize how many of the things we spent so much time worrying about were the wrong things and weren't worth the time and effort. So often we have heard the cliché "You can't take it with you." When we give away what we have instead of hoarding it, we suddenly experience the abundance we do have. In *The Giving Heart*, M. J. Ryan concludes, "that most of us who live in Western societies have a great deal, and when we share what we have, we begin to feel our abundance. It becomes real to us and diminishes our fears."[47]

Why Aren't We More Generous?

God wants us to be a blessing to others, to share what we have with those in need. In a sermon delivered in October 2009 at the Mt. Zion Methodist Church in Cornelius, North Carolina, Tim Reimer suggested that we struggle with generosity at times for two reasons: the voice of fear and the voice of self-gratification.[48] When we struggle to help others, this is typically because one of these two voices is shouting in our heads. We fear that something will happen down the road and we won't be able to pay the bills. Will we have enough left to put food on the table? Because of these fears, we tend not to be generous but to practice "saving." This practice, when taken to the extreme, is "hoarding." Fear of scarcity makes us stingy. We assume generosity may drain our resources. A lifetime of stinginess shrinks our world and tightens our hearts. Stinginess crimps our energy, narrows experiences, shrinks vision, blocks our potential, and closes the doors of life.

The other voice we struggle with is self-gratification. We think that if we give to someone in need, we won't be able to buy what our culture tells us will make us happy. With

---

47   M. J. Ryan, "Secret Benefits of Generosity," grandtimes.com, accessed January 21, 2013, http://www.grandtimes.com/Secret_Benefits.html.

48   Tim Reimer, Sermon Text, October 11, 2009.

so much to buy that society tells us we must have, we don't want to miss out on all the fun. So we aren't generous. We defeat this voice when we are content with what we have and are able to tune out the voices of our culture. We can defeat both voices when we learn the difference between the things we think we need but only desire and the things we actually do need to live. When we learn to distinguish "needs" from "wants," we are free to be generous.

The Significance of Generosity

The prophet Isaiah observed that when we help others, our lights will shine out from the darkness, and the darkness around us shall be as bright as the noonday sun. And the Lord will guide us continually, satisfy us with all good things, and keep us healthy too; and we will be like a well-watered garden, like an ever-flowing spring. When we freely give, we do not deplete our resources but rather replenish them with an ever-flowering spring. The Sanskrit proverb says, "He who allows his day to pass by without practicing generosity and enjoying life's pleasures is like a blacksmith's bellows—he breathes but does not live."

Too often we do our giving for the wrong reasons; aiding someone in need is not a generous act but rather an act that fortifies our egos. We usually do these acts in the open and with a great deal of fanfare and publicity, but when we are generous in secret, we stimulate our souls. In an article "Generous People," Chuck Gallozzi suggests, "The greater the generosity, the greater the joy experienced by both the giver and the receiver. When do we offer "great" generosity? It is when we give more than we imagine we can. Also, when we give what cannot be replaced, we prove that those in need have a higher value than possessions. Finally, when we are sensitive to the needs of others, we will be more concerned with the timing of our gift than the size of it."[49] We get a little lift when we give, don't we? Whenever we go out of our way to help or encourage someone, we feel encouraged and positive toward ourselves. Something happens inside. Even if someone hasn't given to us directly, what does it feel like if we call this person to mind? There is warmth and delight. That's how we regard people who are generous. It's good for us and good for others. We also practice generosity to free others, to extend welfare and happiness to all beings, to somehow, as much as each of us can, lessen the suffering in this world. "When do we experience the greatest act of generosity?" Gallozzi asks. "When we give what cannot be replaced, we prove that the person in need has a higher value than possessions."

Speaking from the Buddhist perspective, Sharon Salzberg claims, "When our practice of generosity is genuine, when it is complete, we realize inner spaciousness and peace, and we also learn to extend boundless caring to all living beings."[50] In her review of this subject, Salzberg writes, "The cultivation of generosity is the beginning of spiritual awakening in our lives." This awakening is a tremendous force arising from an inner capability to let go. "Being able to let go, to give up, to renounce, and then to give generously all spring from the

49   Chuck Gallozzi, "Generous People," personal-development.com, April 22, 2009, http://www.personal-development.com/chuck/generosity.htm.

50   Sharon Salzberg, "Generosity's Perfection," *Shambhala Sun*, March 2005, http://www.shambhalasun.com/index.php?option=content&task=view&id=1304.

same inner source, and when we practice generosity, we open these qualities within ourselves. Letting go gives us profound freedom and many loving ways to express that freedom."

If living generously is so smart, why isn't everyone doing it? Because it isn't easy. You would think everyone would see the wisdom in making investments that have lasting returns and such positive, practical payoffs, but being generous isn't that simple. Wealth is powerful and deceptive. It can seduce most of us and convince us that giving our selves, our time, and our money in love and generosity is too big a risk to take.

When we give, we develop a feeling of having more than enough. We develop a sense of abundance and begin to feel that we are giving from an infinite supply. Knowing that we have more than enough gives us a sense of freedom, a freedom to live more authentically; we live in greater happiness. This sense of freedom allows us to reflect on the good things we've done and take delight in them. As we recall our acts of generosity, we do so not to bolster our egos but rather to acknowledge that we cared enough about ourselves and others to choose to give rather than to hold on. This sense of freedom or abundance also involves awareness, not only of the other person, to see what he needs, but also of ourselves. We can look inward before, during, and after acts of generosity to see ourselves more clearly and to step toward greater freedom, a freedom that feels like a breath of fresh air. Letting go gives us profound freedom and many loving ways to express that freedom.

Caroline V. Clarke says it succinctly: "Generosity is one of the basic laws of nature: give and you shall receive.

It's a biblical notion, a spiritual cornerstone, and a moral imperative."[51] We were created to give, to be a blessing to others. Why should we give? Because we can. Hear Paul's words to Timothy: "We are to be generous and ready to share so that we may experience the life that really is worth living" (1Timothy 6:17-19). Generosity gives significance and meaning to our lives. These feelings of gratitude and generosity are also helpful in solidifying our relationships with people we care about, benefiting the one giving as well as the one receiving.

I leave you with two questions to ponder: How have your acts of generosity affected your family, your community, and your world? What is the legacy of your acts of generosity? If you are unhappy with the answers, it's not too late to make some mid-life changes. Do you have the courage to make these changes? It isn't necessary to travel far to practice generosity. Begin at home by giving moral support to parents, spouses, children, and siblings. Then extend your generosity to the workplace, your communities, and the world at large. One last thought: God measures generosity not by the size of the gift but by the size of the sacrifice.

Exercises in Generosity

- Cultivate everyday generous habits. Look for chances to be an encourager; take time to thank and encourage someone else for what he or she is doing. Business writer Michael Zigarelli described a practice whereby he placed five coins in his pocket at the beginning of

---

51   Caroline V. Clarke, "Be Selfish: Serve Others," *Black Enterprise*, July 1, 2003, http://www.blackenterprise.com/mag/be-selfish-serve-others/.

the day; each time he gave someone a compliment or praised him, he moved one coin over to his other pocket, attempting to have all the coins transferred by the end of the day.[52]

- Share what you have. Look for opportunities to share your time, expertise, and finances for the benefit of others. Determine what causes interest you and invest your time volunteering or supporting these causes financially.

- Advocate for justice. Be informed about injustices that are happening around the world or in your own communities. Actively pursue solutions to these problems by writing to your representatives, letting them know that you expect the government to deal justly and fairly with those in need.

- Practice generosity through promoting peace. Offering forgiveness and grace to others can be a powerfully generous step that will lead to reconciliation in your life and in your relationships with others.

- Make a list of the factors you are thankful for. We take so much for granted. You will be surprised by all that you have—material things, relationships, job, freedom, beliefs, and many other things.

- Express your gratitude. How do you treat people in service capacities—your waitress, parking attendant, grocery store bagger? When someone does a good job, do you acknowledge it?

---

52 David Kilgour, "The Power of Generosity: To Promote Transformation," david-kilgour.com, accessed January 21, 2013, http://www.david-kilgour.com/mp/Generosity.htm.

CHAPTER 7

Integrity

It is well to think well. It is divine to act well.

— HORACE MANN

What Does Integrity Really Look Like?

I've always been a visual learner; visual images seem to make a more powerful impression than words alone on my ability "to see" ideas and concepts. Pictures and images seem to activate my heart and engage me more emotionally. This is especially true about the word *integrity*. Chuck Gallozzi gives us that picture. In his discussion of "Examples of Integrity," he tells the reader,

> If you lived in an arid land, imagine your disappointment when the dark clouds you saw and the howling wind you felt brought no rain. Is the disappointment no less when people in our lives fail to live up to their promises? That's why it is written in the Book of Proverbs, "People who promise things they never give are like clouds and wind that bring no rain" (Proverbs 25:14). This image deals with integrity. Individuals with integrity have unshakable character. They earn our trust and respect. They also have a good reputation because they are reliable and responsible.[53]

There is little question in my assessment of the values of fulfilled lives that those who have learned to practice integrity will lead more significant and rewarding lives. They have learned that to achieve a life of significance they must value consistency in their actions, values, methods, measures, principles, and expectations. Their lives are a reflection of honesty and truthfulness. Wikipedia defines *integrity* as the opposite of hypocrisy; it is the inner sense of "wholeness" deriving from qualities such as honesty and consistency of character.[54] As such, one may judge that

---

53   Chuck Gallozzi, "Examples of Integrity," personal-development. com, April 20, 2009, http://www.personal-development.com/chuck/ integrity.htm.

54   "Integrity," Wikipedia, accessed January 31, 2013, http:// en.wikipedia.org/wiki/Integrity.

others "have integrity" to the extent that they act according to the values, beliefs, and principles they claim to hold. Their actions speak as loudly as their words. Integrity is about principle-centered living. It is about what is right rather than what is expedient. We demonstrate significance when we are the good person we appear to be. For this reason, Socrates taught that "the greatest way to live with honor in this world is to be what we pretend to be."

The root of the word *integrity* is *integer*; an integer is simply a whole number as opposed to a fraction or a part of a number. *Integrity* conveys a sense of wholeness and consistency in your life as opposed to an appearance of separate parts. You are the same person whether you are with your family or spouse, at work or at school, with friends, or at church. A significant life requires that you integrate your values and beliefs into all aspects of your life, in everything you do or say. Integrity combines your ideals, convictions, standards, beliefs, and behaviors. When your behavior matches your values, and when your ideals and actions are in sync, you have integrity. You can't expect to have integrity if you're honest in three or four situations but dishonest in another. The impact of integrity should be visible first in your relationships, second in your marriage, and third in your job.

The Impact of Integrity on Relationships

One of the primary areas of our lives, where acting with integrity is crucial, is in our relationships with our families and friends, the people closest to us. Being true to ourselves means living in truth with each person in our lives. It means refusing to say or do something we don't believe is right. Living in truth with other people means we refuse to stay in any situation where we are unhappy with the behavior of another person. We refuse to tolerate it or to compromise. Psychologists have determined that most stress and negativity comes from attempting to live in a way that is not congruent with our highest values. When we decide to become individuals of character and integrity, our first actions should be to neutralize or remove all difficult relationships from our lives.

"If your enemy is hungry, give him food to eat; if he is thirsty, give him water to drink" (Prov. 25:21). Is this how we live our lives? My guess is that most of us are familiar with this verse, yet many of us who claim to have high levels of integrity every day pass by those we consider to be our enemies without even giving a daily greeting.

With the definitions of integrity we presented earlier, we can readily see that living one's life with integrity is not easy, especially in our relationships. Forces that make living with moral consistency, honesty, and truthfulness difficult continuously bombard us. Most of us have a sense of what living our lives with integrity would mean; we have a picture of our "ideal self" in our minds. Yet we frequently find ourselves falling short of that ideal. In his book *The Six Pillars of Self-Esteem*, Nathaniel Branden concludes that when we behave in ways that conflict with our judgment about what is appropriate, we lose faith in ourselves and respect ourselves less. If we do that repeatedly, we will trust ourselves less or cease to trust ourselves at all, and our self-esteem will suffer. He continues, "When a breach of integrity wounds our self-esteem, only the practice of integrity can heal it."[55]

An ability to feel secure and confident in our capabilities and in the direction of our lives is a must in our relationships. Yet too often we undermine ourselves by judging ourselves harshly or by comparing ourselves with others. We often allow the standards of the world to challenge our feelings of self-worth. For example, a feeling of worth based on adherence to principles of the gospel — kindness, warmth, and faithfulness — is often undermined by a culture that celebrates winning rather than participating, wealth rather than thrift, fame rather than honor, and success rather than service.

We will not always be right or do the right thing in our relationships, but when we have integrity, we will accept responsibility for our wrong actions and feel remorse; we will understand what went wrong and why it happened so we can put a plan in place to ensure it won't happen again. These paths all lead to a life that not only provides us with personal significance but also allows us to breathe greater significance into our relationships.

Marital Integrity

Although the surfeit of examples of infidelity in the news media might erroneously lead us to believe that unfaithfulness is limited to the famous (or infamous) and applies only

---

55   Nathaniel Branden, *Six Pillars of Self-Esteem* (New York: Random House, 1995), quoted in Neil Rosenthal, "Integrity Is Within Your Control," heartrelationships.com, accessed January 21, 2013, http://heartrelationships.com/article/integrity-within-your-control.

to husbands, in fact, a recent survey cited by J. Blair Brown revealed that at least 25 percent of men have relationships outside of their "main" one (compared with just 17 percent of women). The survey also revealed that 65 percent of marriages that break up do so because of adultery.[56] Whether you call it cheating, unfaithfulness, adultery, an affair, or marital infidelity, it causes devastating pain and major crises in marriages. The causes of infidelity are numerous and may be simple or complicated, occurring in both happy and unhappy marriages.

A blog recently defined *marital integrity* as a relationship in which one's words and actions align between husband and wife. "Integrity speaks of wholeness and completeness, where the exterior is made of the same stuff as the interior. It's solid all the way through."[57] Proverbs regularly refers to the wisdom and protection that occur when a person has integrity. For instance, Proverbs 11:3 says, "The integrity of the upright guides them, but the unfaithful are destroyed by their duplicity." The significant person embraces his or her marriage in both word and deed, a loving way to walk in integrity.

Everyone probably agrees that it is not good to promise to be faithful to another person during the wedding ceremony and then later break that promise. Nor is it good when a person plays the part of being married while he or she is not actually married. In both cases actions are not in proper

---

56   J. Blair Brown, "Male Infidelity — When 'Boys Will Be Boys,'" *Regal Magazine*, April 1, 2010, http://www.regalmag.com/male-infidelity-married-a-462.html.

57   Eric Asp, "The Goodness of Marriage — Integrity," *Eric Asp* (blog), June 1, 2011, http://www.ericasp.com/blog.php/2011/06/01/the-goodness-of-marriage-integrity.

alignment. I would contend that both instances demonstrate the same lack of integrity.

Early in their relationship couples need to discuss the moral principles that will govern their relationship. What are the relationship's spoken and unspoken moral guidelines? What are the things the couple has decided not to do? The problem with many marriages today is that the couple lacks a sense of moral guidance. They do not realize that for a marriage to work effectively, it needs to be governed by strong principles; otherwise both parties might be led astray by words or actions, and engage in practices that in the long run are detrimental to an effective marriage relationship. Couples need to be on the same page when it comes to morals and integrity. If people believe they aren't accountable to anyone, they run the risk of doing whatever they want in their marriage; their marriages then lack a sense of moral integrity. In addition, many couples fail to create an environment that fosters integrity governed by moral principles.

Many people today advocate a swinger's lifestyle. Being a player is seen as being cool. This type of coolness flies in the face of living a significant life; it is the worst sort of ego gratification. People aren't trophies to be captured or a big game to be bagged. We must live by certain issues of honor and ethics to truly feel good about ourselves, and the same issues occur in a relationship. The presence of ethics and honor in a relationship involves the practice of loyalty, wisdom, insight, discipline, and integrity: the strength of will to do what one says one will do.

Professional Integrity

You can't control many things in life. You can't control what people say or think about you. You can't control decisions prospective clients make. You can't control your competitors' marketing tactics. You can't control the economy, the stock market, or the weather. However, in the midst of an ever-changing and uncertain environment, you have absolute control over one thing — your integrity. You may think you have little control over your integrity — that your character is hereditary, like eye color or intelligence, and you may believe integrity is a function of your environment. Indeed, heredity, environment, and culture influence your character. Nonetheless, your attitudes and behavior are ultimately yours to control. They are your responsibility, and others, especially in your work space, will judge you accordingly.

Margaret Thorsborne, the managing director of Transformative Justice in Australia, is internationally recognized as an expert on school and workplace bullying and restorative behavior management practices. In a chapter in *The Seven Heavenly Virtues of Leadership*, she discusses the responses she received to a question she asked a group of professionals (CEOs, middle and senior managers, and staff at large and small organizations). The question was, "Think of a boss, manager, leader or someone in your life who you think has integrity. What does that mean to you?" One thing stood out; each person could name only a handful of people he or she believed had integrity. But they could remember plenty of instances where integrity was absent, and they spoke feelingly of the resultant damage to themselves, others, and the organization.[58]

Has integrity become an old-fashioned virtue? The world these days seems to be full of stories about its absence. Integrity has become a low priority somewhere in the quest for increasing profit, market share, votes, and tenure. These are the words respondents in the above study used when asked to describe the people they identified as possessing integrity.

- Strength of character
- Steadfast, resolute, having fiber
- Walking the talk, doing what was promised
- Authentic, straightforward; what's on the inside is displayed on the outside.
- Open, honest, and direct in their dealings with others
- Clear and uncompromised values, clarity about what's right and wrong
- Committed, having the courage of their convictions
- Behaviors matched values (congruence)
- Principled, honorable, fair, accountable, and responsible
- Balanced, integrated, whole
- Self-aware and self-reflective
- Mature and wise

People characterized by the above descriptors don't live divided lives; their morals, ethics, and treatment of others are the same wherever they are and whatever they're doing.

---

58 Margaret Thorsborne, *The Seven Heavenly Virtues of Leadership.* (Australia: Australia Institute of Management, 1998-2008).

Integrity, as a functional element of leadership, crosses all boundaries for these individuals.

To be truly successful, you must have great personal integrity. Although you may know people who seem to profit from personal treachery or shady dealings, their success is unlikely to last. Integrity is critical to maximize career advancement; you must be trustworthy, ethical, honest, dependable to the core, and, most important, consistent. Others glimpse your personal integrity through your behavior, reputation, lifestyle, scruples, morals, ethics, and personal and social maturity.

Most religions of the world have a rule that is almost identical with the Christian Golden Rule. These are universally transferable, fundamental truths about how we should treat people. When you follow the Golden Rule and live with integrity, you set an example that has a far greater impact than any words you could speak. If you want to push your people to a new performance level, get motivated to grow and develop yourself. Remember, your people will do what they see you do. Significance can be contagious!

Jack Welsh once warned that if you state one thing in a corporate meeting and then do something else afterward, "You're dead!" To lead by example, you need integrity to do what you suggest others do. In *Good to Great*, Jim Collins points out that most great CEOs are humble people who lead a balanced life and are inclusive of the people around them. Being in their presence makes others want to be better.[59]

---

59   Jim Collins, *Good to Great: Why Some Companies Make the Leap... and Others Don't* (New York: HarperCollins, 2001).

Significance of Integrity

Lack of personal integrity — in other words, not being completely truthful and honest in all areas of life — is probably one of the greatest causes of stress and unhappiness we can have. Yet, strangely, it is hardly ever mentioned as a cause of stress. Few people doubt that truthfulness is liberating. When we speak or act in truth and honesty, we feel good; we feel at peace with ourselves. This is why people who have held onto a "dark" secret much of their lifetimes feel so liberated and free when they finally confess. That's why the well-known biblical aphorism "The truth shall set you free" (John 8:32) is as profound and real today as it was when Jesus stated it two thousand years ago.

As we view contemporary society, how often do we observe examples of jealousy, envy, and greed accompanied by pretense, denial, and dishonesty? These are the dysfunctional systems for our underlying feelings of insecurity and powerlessness. We use alcohol, drugs, overwork, and infidelity to numb these feelings. We see how this lack of integrity interferes with our attempts to be authentic, destroying our credibility in our relationships with friends, at work, and in our marriages. In *The Leadership Integrity Challenge* Ed Morler describes these contemporaries as "chronically angry, confused, afraid, defensive, depressed, despairing, apathetic, shallow, work obsessed, burned out or wanting to drop out."[60] When integrity ceases to be a primary standard, the true costs are beyond measure.

---

60 Ed Morler, *The Leadership Integrity Challenge: Accessing and Facilitating Emotional Maturity* (Tel Aviv, Israel: Sinai Publishing, 2006).

Exercises in Integrity

- Invest your time, love, effort, and money in places, people, and businesses that match your own integrity.
- Surround yourself with people who are complementary to your skills and abilities, and who operate from the same level of integrity you do.
- Awareness exercise: Pay attention to the following:

  - ✓ How often you break rules, even if no one notices it
  - ✓ How often you break your promises, no matter how small or insignificant they are
  - ✓ How often you are not at your best in any role you assigned yourself to fill
  - ✓ How often you do not fulfill another's expectations

- Learn to like yourself. Look in the mirror each day and say something positive about yourself. Praise and reward yourself for jobs well done. Compliment yourself for good ideas. Praise yourself for the strength you possess and resolve to attain the strengths you need to develop further.
- Bring enthusiasm to everything you do. Enthusiasm is critical to success in everything you do, not only for yourself, but also for those around you. Enthusiasm draws others to you. Positive energy is always contagious.
- Make your word your bond. Be a person who does what he says he will do. Be a person others know they can count on.

- Develop a personal code of ethics. Establish your own code of ethics and be willing to hold your ground in living by it regardless of temptation or cost. Let others know what standards you live by and do not disappoint them or yourself.
- Describe an experience or event when you demonstrated integrity.
- In your relations with friends, family, and coworkers, find ways to validate, listen to, take seriously, and respect others' negative views or feelings. Refrain from "blowing people off." When we truly listen to people and take them seriously, they feel understood and valued, and we minimize the negative effect.
- Seven tips for developing integrity:

  - ✓ Value integrity.
  - ✓ Talk about integrity.
  - ✓ Find an integrity mentor.
  - ✓ Seek feedback.
  - ✓ Examine your heart.
  - ✓ Be courageous.
  - ✓ Walk your talk.

CHAPTER 8

Service to Others

If you want to lift yourself up, lift up someone else.

— BOOKER T. WASHINGTON

Community Service and Volunteerism

In 1984, I was invited to become a member of a local Rotary club. As part of the club's orientation, I noted that the club is a "service club," and its primary focus is to provide opportunities for members to support service projects, volunteering their efforts in support of local and worldwide projects. Rotary's motto is, in fact, "Service Above Self." Since that date, I have contributed in various volunteer roles, ranging from building ramps for the handicapped, tutoring, and bell ringing for the Salvation Army to raising funds to support the worldwide effort to eliminate polio. As a result of this orientation, I view the terms *volunteerism* and *service* to be synonymous.

Many challenges face our nation—homelessness, pollution, poverty, hunger, substance abuse, broken families, and more. Service is one of the best ways, if not *the* best way, to see the positive impact our actions can have on these situations and the broken lives around us. Whether you volunteer in a retirement home, teach someone to read, serve as a counselor, build a house for a family in need, or organize a bone-marrow drive service, *your* service can change the world.

To most people, a volunteer is someone who contributes time primarily to helping others with no expectation of pay or other material benefit to himself or herself. Our communities and their clubs and organizations abound with opportunities to serve. Nonprofit organizations, in particular, need volunteers to lend their expertise in a variety of ways—administration, counseling, painting, cooking, gardening, teaching, ministering, and more.

Volunteering in the United States

A philanthropic spirit has been a part of our American tradition since the first pioneers arrived on our eastern shores. Many historians believe these early colonists had to establish support systems to survive the many challenges that came with living in their new land. From farming the land to dealing with devastating diseases, togetherness was vital for survival; helping one another was a lesson learned by the first settlers and remembered by future generations.

This spirit continued throughout the Revolutionary War, when volunteers joined forces to raise funds for the war effort. It was vital to the foundation of the Salvation Army, which moved through the tenement districts in New York City and other large cities, caring for the poor in the 1900s. During the Great Depression in the 1930s, volunteers were mobilized to assist millions of people who were unemployed, hungry, and homeless. World Wars I and II brought out volunteers to support both servicemen and civilians in a variety of areas. And in the 1960s, volunteerism focused on a different kind of war — a liberal one — working against poverty, inequality, and violence at home and around the world. The history of volunteerism in America can be chronicled today in a generation of new causes, including green living, animal welfare, equal rights, and gender and sexual orientation.

The US Bureau of Labor Statistics has detailed our more recent history of volunteerism in America. For example, they report that the rate of volunteerism declined by .5 percentage point to 26.3 percent of the US population for the year ending in September 2010. About 62.8 million people volunteered through or for an organization at least once between September 2009 and September 2010. The volunteer rate in 2010 was similar to the rate observed in 2007 and 2008. The volunteer rate for women decreased from 30.1 percent to 29.3 percent in the year ending September 2010, while the rate for men, at 23.2 percent, was essentially unchanged. Statistically, the age-group of thirty-five-year-olds to forty-four-year-olds was most likely to volunteer (32.2 percent). Persons in their early twenties were least likely to volunteer (18.4 percent).[61]

Among the major race and ethnic groups, whites continued to volunteer at a higher rate (27.8 percent) than did blacks (19.4 percent) and Asians (19.6 percent). The volunteer rates of whites and blacks declined from the prior year. Among Hispanics or Latinos, 14.7 percent volunteered in 2010, the same rate as 2009. Married persons, individuals with higher levels of education, and employed groups also demonstrated higher levels of volunteerism. In 2010, the groups for which the volunteers worked the most hours during the year were most frequently religious groups (33.8 percent of all volunteers), followed by educational or youth service-related groups (26.5 percent). Another 13.6 percent of volunteers performed activities mainly for social or community service organizations.

The Corporation for National and Community Service has estimated that the economic value of all this volunteerism in 2009 was $169 billion. To put this in context, this is roughly equivalent to the 2009 GDP of the state of Alabama. On the surface, this appears to be an impressive effort on the part of our nation, but in reality only one in five Americans is reaching out to help others through some type of volunteer service.[62]

---

61   U.S. Department of Labor, Bureau of Labor Statistics, "Volunteering in 2010," TED: The Editor's Desk, January 28, 2011, http://www.bls.gov/opub/ted/2011/ted_20110128.htm.

62   Ricardo Azziz, "1 in 5: The Importance of Volunteerism," *Sculpting in Clay: Reflections on Leadership and Transformation* (blog), May 19, 2011, http://azziz.georgiahealth.edu/archives/266.

Why People Volunteer

From the first volunteer fire department Benjamin Franklin founded in 1736 to the establishment of Vista and the Peace Corps in the 1960s to the national service legislation signed by President Obama in 2010, Americans have long demonstrated a willingness to volunteer. People volunteer for a variety of reasons. Most often they volunteer because they need or want to help others. They tend to enjoy a sense of satisfaction and personal fulfillment as a result of their participation in some type of volunteer experience. Others have more self-serving motives and join various groups for the benefits they produce (see the next section on Benefits of Volunteering). Some people consider this latter motive selfish and hypocritical, a reaction that may be derived from the long tradition of seeing volunteering as a form of charity.

Although the best volunteering does involve the desire to serve others, other motives should not be excluded. Susan J. Ellis, president of Energize, Inc., suggests that instead of considering volunteering as something you do for others not as fortunate as yourself, you begin to think of it as "an exchange." She suggests that we "consider that most people find themselves in need at some point in their lives. So today you may be the person with the ability to help, but tomorrow you may be the recipient of someone else's volunteer effort. Even now you might be on both sides of the service cycle; maybe you are a tutor for someone who can't read, while last week the volunteer ambulance medic rushed you to the emergency room. Volunteerism also includes 'self-help'; if you are active in your neighborhood crime watch, your home is protected while you protect your neighbors' homes.

Adding your effort to the work of others makes everyone's lives better."[63]

The Benefits of Volunteering

Volunteering is important for numerous reasons and benefits both the community and the volunteers themselves. Volunteerism is a two-way street; it can benefit you and your family as much as the cause you choose to help. Researchers often refer to the sense of exhilaration that occurs in volunteers as "helpers high."

Dedicating your time as a volunteer helps you meet a diverse range of people and make new friends. This is especially true if you are new to an area. Volunteerism strengthens your ties to the community, broadens your support systems, and exposes you to people with common interests and neighborhood resources. These social interactions also provide opportunities to boost your self-confidence, self-esteem, and life satisfaction. By doing good for others, you gain a sense of pride and identity.

Volunteering also provides opportunities to gain experiences in a particular area of interest that may be helpful in looking for a new career or pursuing an avocational interest you have always wanted to investigate. Volunteer situations may also provide opportunities to practice workplace skills, such as oral and written communication, ability to work with others, ability to take directions, leadership skills, and task and time management.

---

[63] Susan J. Ellis, "Why Volunteer?" Energize Inc., accessed January 22, 2013, http://www.energizeinc.com/art/awhy.html.

In all of this it is important to remember that volunteering is not all work! It can be a relaxing, energizing escape from the routine of work or school.

Significance of Serving

As if the benefits of volunteering just cited were insufficient, research lends convincing support to the theory that volunteering leads to a longer, more fulfilling life. A growing body of social science research measures rewards beyond the psychological rewards of volunteering. Richard Adler in *Aging Today* concludes that "volunteerism goes well beyond just making the participants feel better about themselves, it helps them stay healthy and may even prolong their lives."[64] According to researcher Neenah L. Chappel, studies demonstrate that 70 percent of older volunteers claim to enjoy a better quality of life than the average non-volunteer.[65] A survey by the Seniors Research Group found that 52 percent of elders who volunteer frequently say they are very satisfied with life compared to 45 percent of occasional volunteers and only 37 percent of non-volunteers.[66] Research has also found that when patients with chronic or serious illness volunteer, they receive benefits beyond what can be achieved through medical care.

In Canada, an Ontario study of volunteers linked to health benefits found that volunteerism not only improved

---

64 Richard Adler, "The Volunteer Factor," *Aging Today*, 25, no. 4 (July — August 2004), accessed January 22, 2013, http://civicventures. org/publications/articles/the_volunteer_factor.cfm.

65 Ibid.

66 Ibid.

self-esteem but also reduced social isolation, lowered blood pressure, and enhanced the immune system.[67] Furthermore, a study on volunteerism and mortality revealed that older adults who volunteer actually experience a lower mortality rate. A study performed at the University of Michigan Research Center supports this finding. The study tracked volunteers who had histories of heart conditions and found that they experienced reduced chest pain and lower cholesterol levels. Also, men who volunteer at least once a week lived longer than men who did not volunteer. A wealth of other varied research documents that volunteering reduces anxiety and depression, increases mental functioning, decreases insomnia, speeds recovery from surgery, increases energy, and leads to more successful weight control.[68]

These findings are particularly relevant today since baby boomers — the generation of seventy-seven million Americans born after World War II are reaching the age typically associated with retirement. We know baby boomers in their late forties and fifties are volunteering at a higher rate than earlier generations at the same age did. Maintaining and increasing these levels of volunteering will not only help solve many community problems but also simultaneously enhance the health of the growing number of older adults. This brief review of the research leaves little doubt that many benefits derived from doing volunteer work reach

---

67 Judy Looman Swinson, "Focusing on the Health Benefits of Volunteering as a Recruitment Strategy," *The International Journal of Volunteer Administration,* 24, no. 2 (October 2006): 25 – 30.

68 Ibid.

far beyond the volunteer act itself and may linger long after the volunteer role is relinquished.

Once again we ask the question, what gives significance to our lives? Is it money, property, a successful career, a big car, an attractive spouse? Most would agree that these things in themselves do not add *lasting* and *profound* meaning to our lives. Albert Einstein said that only a life lived for others is a life worthwhile, and I believe a life of service to others is what truly brings meaning to our lives — not the deed that brings a return for an equal or similar deed but unselfish kindness and generosity, acts that validate our good fortune. It is those acts that give meaning to our lives and, above all, sustain and dignify the lives of others. Do not squander the moments in your life when you are given the opportunity to make a difference in the lives of others.

In our quest for the marks of a significant life, we must not bypass the quality that so completely characterized the life of Jesus, the quality of unselfish servanthood. Jesus said, "For even the Son of Man did not come to be served but to serve, and to give his life as a ransom for many" (Mark 10:45). There is no question that if we are concerned with living a significant life, we must experience progress in giving of ourselves to and for others. Servant living stands opposed to the primary concerns we see today, where the focus of our culture and society is more on our own personal happiness and comfort.

Exercises in Service to Others

- Think about how much you receive when you give and list some of the reasons you want to volunteer.

- Think back on a time in your life when you were being served. How did it help you? What did you think of those who served you? How did you treat them?
- Express your appreciation. Though you recognize that volunteer work is often much more beneficial to you, saying "thanks" for the opportunity to serve is something far too few people do.
- Volunteer with your family. Get your family involved in one of the National Days of Service, such as Make a Difference Day or Martin Luther King Jr. Day. Spend a day painting murals or cleaning your neighborhood park.
- Find your inner hero. Have you dreamed of being a doctor or firefighter? You can check out opportunities to volunteer at local hospitals and fire departments to get a glimpse of what community heroes are doing. Make a difference as part of their team.
- There's no need to wait to be asked. There are many ways to find organizations that are looking for volunteers. Ask your friends or colleagues about their own volunteering activities. The Internet offers great online volunteer referral services, including Volunteer.gov. Or try visiting your local volunteer center. These services can help you find the right volunteer opportunity for you.
- Think outside the box! Many community groups looking for volunteers for neighborhood watch programs, prisons, disaster relief organizations, youth organizations, intergenerational programs, and park services may not have occurred to you, but they could be the perfect fit.

- Research causes or issues that are important to you. Look for a group that deals with issues you feel strongly about.
- Consider letting kids bring their friends. This may make the service experience more fun for them, and it could inspire more families to get involved in volunteering.
- Look for opportunities that can accommodate the skills, interests, and maturity of all family members, especially the younger children.

CHAPTER 9

Perseverance

Perseverance is the hard work you do after the hard work you already did.

— NEWT GINGRICH

What Is Perseverance?

I love old adages; I use them every day, especially when the grandkids are around. Two of my favorites are the following:

- When the going gets tough, the tough get going.
- It's not your *aptitude* but your *attitude* that determines your *altitude* in life.

Who wrote these or where they came from, I have no idea, but I'm grateful they're in my trove. These two adages are especially relevant to this chapter on perseverance.

A definition of perseverance usually includes the concepts of pursuing worthy objectives with determination and patience, and demonstrating fortitude when confronted with failure. Do you find the words *pursuing*, *determination*, *patience*, and *fortitude* challenging? They make my blood flow. Perseverance is often the personal trait that makes the difference between success and failure. This trait of perseverance provides such strong physical, psychological, social, and spiritual benefits; some would say it gives an "indomitable spirit." This is why it is almost always included on professionals' lists of the "most desired" character traits.

"Perseverance is failing 19 times and succeeding the 20th," according to Julie Andrews, "It means having the attitude no matter what, no matter when, no matter how." It means setting your mind to a goal and doing everything in your power to achieve it. For those in the older age group, life today sometimes seems to be all about instant gratification—wanting it all now and doing it the easy way. We, who are part of the "greatest generation" have come to realize that the things we appreciate most are the things we worked the hardest and longest for. In the days of microwave ovens, fast food, cell phones, and instant messaging, this lesson may be hard to learn.

Kathleen Barton, a workshop presenter and life coach, claims that those who persevere have certain qualities; in particular, they have a compelling sense of purpose that drives them to succeed. Purpose is their reason for being: it's why they exist. Barton cites a second quality of persevering people — "belief in yourself." These individuals are confident they can do it. She states, "If you are determined and believe you can succeed, you are more than halfway to achieving your goal."[69] I really prefer the word *grit* to *perseverance*. It provides an image that adds a sense of passion for life's goals. Grit is conceptualized as a trait that does not require immediate positive feedback. Often, "gritty" individuals do not seek fame or external recognition for their achievements. They do not seek to distinguish themselves from other people in pursuit of their personal goals.

Those who have cultivated the habit of perseverance seem to enjoy insurance against failure. No matter how many times they are defeated, they keep going until they finally arrive toward the top of the ladder. In *Think and Grow Rich*, Napoleon Hill observed men like Henry Ford, who started from scratch and built an industrial empire of huge proportions, with little else in the way of advantage but persistence. Another example is Thomas A. Edison, who, with less than three months of schooling, became the world's leading inventor and converted persistence into the talking machine, the incandescent light bulb, plus about fifty or so other useful inventions. Edison

---

69 Kathleen Barton, "The Power of Perseverance," yourlifebalance-coach.com, accessed January 21, 2013, http://www.yourlifebalance-coach.com/files/The%20Power%20of%20Perseverance.pdf

declared, "I have not failed. I've just found ten thousand ways that don't work."[70] We need the same persistence to keep going. Failure is never fatal.

Teaching Perseverance?

We began this chapter with a couple of my favorite old adages. I'd like to add another:

- It's not what's *taught* that's important, but what is *caught*.

The "catching" kids do while growing up is probably the most successful vehicle for inculcating this trait. Parents are challenged to ingrain the value of perseverance into their children. They must instill the value of never quitting and always giving things their best shot. They should encourage kids to always look at the positive side and find the good in the situation rather than dwell on the bad. Kids should be encouraged to see the problems of their lives as challenges, and the challenges as opportunities for success. Giving up is very easy when things don't go our way. We've all been in situations where a missed opportunity discouraged us and made it difficult to persevere. Life is full of challenges. Nevertheless, it's important that we improve our perseverance and keep going. Every day we try is another chance for success, and giving up is no longer an option.

---

70 Napoleon Hill, *Think and Grow Rich* (Toronto: Random House, 1960), 2.

These attitudes can be applied to challenges on the athletic field, in the classroom, or in interactions with peers. Winning isn't everything, but we need to foster the winning attitude as we rear our children. At the same time, our kids can't be afraid to fail; through failing we gain a wealth of experience and wisdom. Like the old adage "Get up just one more time than the number of times you have been knocked down," staying with it applies to almost everything that is good and worthwhile in life, from learning to walk to riding a bicycle. Our childhood teaches us that failure occurs only when we stop trying. It's a lesson many of us need to revisit in adulthood.

Harold Stevenson, a professor of psychology at the University of Michigan, conducted one of the most fascinating studies on student achievement. Stevenson sought to answer the question many Americans ask, namely, why do Asian students do better academically than American students? Asian parents strongly stress the value of effort with their children. By expecting their children to work hard and emphasizing no excuses for poor grades, they nurture perseverance in their children. Stevenson also found that American parents place a greater emphasis on children's innate abilities—which tends to lower expectations for their children if they perceive them to have lower academic success.[71]

---

71   Harold Stevenson, "Why Boosting Perseverance Predicts Success More than a Harvard Degree," micheleborba.com, June 25, 2010, http://www.micheleborba.com/blog/2010/06/25/why-perseverance-counts-more-than-a-harvard-degree-focus-on-what-really-matters-mom/.

Learning and Practicing Can Improve Perseverance

Although I tried to make a case for "catching" rather "teaching" perseverance, I believe a case can be made for both, depending on one's station in life. Elizabeth L. Hamilton suggests that learning perseverance requires the exercise of character. "This is," she says, "a character trait, but when learning perseverance, you will need to apply other character traits: commitment, decisiveness, determination, diligence, optimism, patience, persistence, purpose, resourcefulness, responsibility, self-control, and thoroughness."[72] So where do we begin? What must we do? What steps are involved in increasing our perseverance or, as some prefer to call it, our "perseverance quotient" or "personal drive quotient"? The literature is replete with examples of the "how to" for improving the quality of our perseverance. I have attempted to cull this research and cite those methods that appear most meaningful for the purposes of this work.

Motivate Yourself on a Regular Basis

You can help yourself in several ways with daily affirmations, visualizations, journal writing, and inspiring quotes. Overcome the myths that some secret, external force governs your life. For some, this mythical force may be race, religion, gender, upbringing, social class, education, physical features, handicaps, or even parents. Instead of focusing on

---

72   Elizabeth Hamilton, "Learning Thoughts," *Wealthy Thoughts* 7, July 31, 2010, http://www.financial-inspiration.com/Wealthy_Thoughts-wealthy-thoughts-007-learning-perseverance.html.

what you think are your negative qualities, accentuate your strengths and assets.

Analyze Your Mistakes and Correct Them

You should try to learn from each mistake because, if you are forced to repeat them, you'll have the urge to quit, and quitting is not your goal. It is very easy to give up when you make a mistake, but a better choice is to analyze each error so you'll know where you went wrong. That will make it easier for you to connect with your persevering side. Ask yourself the following questions:

- Did I forget a crucial step?
- Did external forces affect my focus?
- Did I prepare myself enough for the challenge?
- Is it a goal I truly wanted to pursue?

Don't Be Rigid—Flexibility and Adaptation to Change Are Important

An inescapable part of learning perseverance is dealing with changes, obstacles, and setbacks. Sometimes changing your course of action is a good thing because when you are too rigid, you may find yourself at a dead end. If your primary plan needs to change to give you a better outcome, make the change. Avoid any circumstance that may make you less able to persevere. As Murphy's Law reminds us, anything that can go wrong will go wrong. You will need to exercise resourcefulness to find your way around roadblocks, and you will need optimism to force yourself over the hurdles.

Bumps in the road will try your patience. Just remember these challenges are all part of learning perseverance.

Seek the Best Source of Advice

When seeking advice, you must consider the source very carefully. If you want to shorten the distance from perseverance to achievement, you will want to learn from the mistakes of others rather than repeating them yourself. You will also want to use the methods that have brought others the success you seek. If you're planning to climb Mt. Everest, who will you look to for advice? The best source is someone who has already done it.

Don't Be Afraid to Take the Road Less Traveled

Be open to experimenting with new ideas. How does this advice help with perseverance? It is easier to keep going when you step outside your comfort zone and find success in many different areas. You become more curious about various outcomes and the risks associated with them, and the surge of adrenaline you feel after taking risks keeps your perseverance quotient elevated.

Examine and Reexamine Your Objective

Sometimes we experience a lack of perseverance because we aim in the wrong direction. If we look more clearly at our goals, we may conclude that our approach needs to be altered. Reexamining our goals is an exercise that may clarify the steps we need to take to keep moving forward.

These steps may actually increase our level of perseverance. Remember that goals are always changing, and that isn't a negative thing as long as we are experiencing progress and success.

Forgive and Forget

Try not to hang onto painful memories and bad feelings. Your past can control you if you don't control it. Forgive past wrongs and move on. Don't forget that forgiving yourself is an important part of the process. Don't let the past determine your future. Forgiving the other person is beneficial to your perseverance. Carrying around the emotions that accompany grudges, disappointments, hatred, or disapproval is toxic to your spirit of perseverance. Instead of lamenting what you didn't or couldn't do, seek inspiration from what you have already achieved and build on that foundation.

Dump the Bad Habits and Thoughts

Being emotionally or mentally rigid means you hang on to habits that no longer serve you, habits that can make you unproductive, frustrated, and unfulfilled while eroding your level of perseverance. Examples of such counterproductive habits are the following:

- Grousing about politics, work, or the neighbors with friends
- Blowing small aggravations out of proportion
- Dwelling in the past

- Worrying about things that may not even happen or that you cannot control
- Worrying about what others are doing or have done
- Viewing yourself as a victim.

Healthy Living

Health is critical because energy and stamina are necessary for perseverance. You need to be at the top level of your game to achieve the focus, resilience, self-confidence, optimism, and clarity needed to be perseverant. Explore the healing power of music, exercise, and pets. When you purchase books, films, and other media for your entertainment, you should seek those with strong uplifting themes. Select those that will nurture your spirit.

The Significance of Perseverance in Life

As I concluded from Hamilton's work (mentioned earlier), learning and practicing perseverance are not activities for the weak of heart. Whenever we are faced with situations that require us to keep going, even when all odds are against us, facing such challenges takes real courage. If we were to put our modesty aside, I'm confident that each of us could relate at least one example of practicing perseverance in our lives, or at least in the lives of those around us. If we still come up short, I'm assured that we have all read about famous people who have demonstrated perseverance in their lives. I'd like to briefly mention a few of the more famous ones.

- Walt Disney: He was fired from his first job because he didn't have any good ideas. You have probably seen a Disney movie and heard about Disney World.
- Ludwig van Beethoven: His own father called him hopeless, but he went on to become a world-famous composer.
- Winston Churchill: He failed the sixth grade. Later he became the prime minister of England.
- Albert Einstein: Einstein couldn't speak until the age of four; he couldn't read until the age of seven. He later discovered the theory of relativity.
- F. W. Woolworth: Woolworth's employers refused to allow him to help customers because he "didn't have enough sense." Woolworth went on to own and operate a large chain of department stores.
- Henry Ford: As a youth, he was evaluated as showing no promise. Ford invented the Model T car.
- Louis Pasteur: A professor gave him a rating of mediocre in chemistry at the Royal College. Pasteur later became a famous bacteriologist and chemist who made many contributions to the world of medicine.
- Louisa May Alcott: An editor told her that her writing would never appeal to the public. She later wrote the novel *Little Women*.
- Isaac Newton: Isaac's work in elementary school was rather poor. He went on to discover the law of gravity.
- Admiral Richard Byrd: He was deemed unfit for military service. Byrd flew over the North and South Poles.

These individuals didn't succumb to the day-to-day decision to give up. They didn't focus on the situations, feelings and challenges that can over time cause us to lose heart and lose our way. When they felt lost, overwhelmed, betrayed, and exhausted, they realized they had a choice about how to respond, and they responded in a manner that brought them success. Mike Bundrant summarizes, "Each of the individuals cited above endured the deepest struggles over many years, quietly (and sometimes not so quietly) dedicated to their cause. Each of them made the world a different place for having persevered. When we remain committed to our own personal cause, in a way we join these and other great spirits in the passionate struggle that often defines life and the human condition."[73]

Are you feeling a little empty? Have these words and examples caused you to reflect on your own life? Have there been too many times when you haven't had your shoulder to the grindstone or walked away from a task undone? Have you disappointed yourself and others or failed to be an example for your kids? Don't lose hope—it's never too late to acquire the skill of perseverance. Acquiring this skill will allow you and those around you to have a more rewarding and enriching life. Failure doesn't have to be an option once you know and practice the elements of perseverance. Commit now to avoid quitting on yourself no matter what.

---

73   Mike Bundrant, "Three Rarely Mentioned Benefits of Perseverance," *Hang in There Blog*, August 3, 2011, http://www.hanginthereblog.com/blog/three-rarely-mentioned-benefits-of-perseverance.html.

Exercises to Build Perseverance in Children

- Replace criticism with encouragement. Instead of nagging or focusing on the negative, replace your criticism with encouragement. You might say, "Maybe if you tried to do (blank) next time, it would be even better" instead of "You didn't do that right." Compliment them on what they have achieved.
- Accept their imperfections. Your kids don't need to be perfect. Make doing their best their ideal. Help them to focus on what they've gained through their experiences and how they can use this success in the future. Avoid focusing on what they didn't do or "should have done" differently. Allow them to make mistakes and forgive themselves. Try laughing along with them instead of criticizing.
- Encourage them to take reasonable risks. Your kids need to understand the old adages "Nothing ventured, nothing gained" and "It is better to have loved and lost than never to have loved at all." Without risk, there's no reward. Risk avoidance dampens the spirit, undermining the will to persist in the face of obstacles. Help them to realize that the choice *not* to choose is probably one of the riskiest choices they can ever make.
- Start a family "never give up" motto. Begin with a family motto such as, "Don't quit until you succeed," "In this family we finish what we start," "Try, try, and try again until you win," or "Quitters never win." Get your kids to write these mottos on index cards and tape them to their bathroom mirrors or in their bedrooms.

- Let them choose what they want to achieve. As much as you want your children to make the honor roll, it's best to let them decide what they want to achieve; then you can help them make a plan. Some goals will require more input from you. If parents find they're nagging or getting angry with their children, and their children aren't working hard enough to meet a goal, that's a signal parents need to back off.

- Teach a child how to go through a task step-by-step. Some children need a lot of structure. You need to help them break a large project, such as a book report or term paper, into smaller tasks so they aren't totally over-whelmed. Encourage them to think of solutions or the best way to do things.

- Be a persevering role model. You are your child's best teacher; show him or her your resilience and deter-mination in the face of difficulties; admit your mis-takes. Model the strategies that get you back on track. Tell your children about your commitment to follow through on the tasks you take on, even when they get difficult. Modeling the trait is always the number one teaching method.

- Have your child write a report on a person of his or her choosing who demonstrated perseverance. Some examples are Albert Einstein, Helen Keller, Thomas Edison, Harriet Tubman, Franklin D. Roosevelt, Mother Teresa, Madame Curie, Ray Charles, Rosa Parks, and Christopher Reeve. Have your children answer the following questions in their report:

- ° How did he/she show perseverance?
- ° In what ways are you like the person in the report?
- ° In what ways are you different from that person?
- ° What did you learn about yourself from writing the report?

- Have your child write something, draw a picture, or use puppets to illustrate a time when he or she persevered and succeeded even though he or she felt like giving up. Then discuss the feelings associated with this achievement—for example, pride, happiness, self-confidence, and self-esteem.
- Have your children create a list of questions they would like to ask an older relative or family friend. For example,

- ° What was the most important thing you learned from your mother or father?
- ° What values are most important in your life today?
- ° What are you most proud of doing?
- ° Name a mistake you once made.
- ° What did you learn from your mistake?
- ° Can you describe when you kept trying, even though you felt like giving up?

CHAPTER 10

The Christian Faith

Come unto me, ye who are weary and overburdened,
and I will give you rest.

— MATTHEW 11:28

A Challenge Ahead

I have approached each chapter with a certain level of trepidation, challenged by the difficulty of explaining why each value is significant to achieving a meaningful life.

This trepidation is maximized in this chapter because this last value may be the one that drives all the others. I'm not suggesting that without it the others are impossible, but with it there appears to be a more natural flow, a congruence that cannot be overlooked. Or perhaps this value may be more "divine" than the others. But then, what could be more divine than being generous or forgiving? Perhaps it's just the thought that this value may be more personal than the others, or just the fact that whenever we deal directly with God, that interaction can be more challenging and intimidating.

But before we move forward, let me remind you that the purpose of this chapter is not to proselytize but rather to share with you my thoughts on how faith can lead to a more significant life.

Religion vs. Faith

Religion and *faith* are two words that are often confused. Strictly speaking, both are different in terms of their concepts and connotations. Many people have faith but do not believe in religion. Religion is man-made, whereas faith is a spiritual concept. Faith is personal and identifies the "strength" of the person, paying homage to whatever it is he or she believes in. Faith is something anyone can believe about anything. You may have faith that your car will start in the morning or that your plane won't crash into the ocean. Faith is a way of believing in the outcome of forces, events, and sciences we do not personally understand. It is a belief with strong conviction, a firm belief in something for which there may be no tangible proof, complete trust in or devotion to something or someone. Faith is the opposite of doubt.

A common and familiar story is told about a group of spectators who watched a high-wire aerialist push a wheelbarrow full of bricks back and forth on a cable above Niagara Falls. When the aerialist asked if anyone in the crowd believed he could do this feat with someone in the wheelbarrow, a man said, "Yes, I believe that you could do that." The aerialist then invited the man to get in. Faith is accepting the invitation to get into the wheelbarrow.

Religion, on the other hand, is the means by which people universally exhibit their faith. Religion is an organized society of people who believe in the existence of a certain god or gods, and who lead their lives in a manner they believe would please that god or gods. Religion is a fundamental set of beliefs and practices a group generally agrees upon. These sets of beliefs concern the cause, nature, and purpose of the universe and involve devotional and ritual observances. They also often contain a moral code governing the conduct of human affairs.

Recently, I completed reading *The Master-Key to Riches*, whose author has an interesting slant to faith: "It lifts humble people to positions of fame, power and fortune. It is the 'eternal elixir' which gives creative power and action to the impulses of thought. Faith is the basis of all so-called miracles, and of many mysteries which cannot be explained by the rules of logic or science. It is the spiritual 'chemical' which, when it is mixed with prayer, gives one direct and immediate connection with one's God. Faith is the power which transmutes the ordinary energies of thought into their spiritual equivalent."[74]

Although we have attempted to describe a distinct difference between the words *faith* and *religion*, in actuality there is often a blending of meaning, for which distinguishing any differences is difficult. This is especially true with some of the research cited below. In addition, distinguishing one from the other in the "blending" that occurs in their lives is often difficult for individuals.

What Is the Christian Faith?

We have all encountered struggles in our lives when we brought forth all our human resources but still fell short of the mark. At times like this we realize we need something we can't do for ourselves. We realize something is out there that we need to tap into, a force that pours into us from an outside source and lodges in our innermost beings. This something has the potential to brighten our lives, direct our senses, and compel our reasoning. Even after you are satisfied with your life, you may still be seeking something else; you may be seeking meaning or purpose to fill a void or yearning you cannot quite explain. This something is faith in God.

The Christian faith is the experience of living in a dynamic and new personal relationship with God through the transforming and indwelling power of Jesus Christ in your body and life. Christianity (from the ancient Greek word *Khristos* or "Christ," literally meaning the "anointed

---

74   Napoleon Hill, *The Master-Key to Riches* (New York: Penguin, 2007), 12.

one") is a monotheistic religion based on the life and teachings of Jesus as presented in the canonical Gospels and other New Testament writings.

A Christian faith shapes our lives, travels all through our being, and redefines who we are. Through this process of integration our faith becomes personal and truly our own. I believe this faith is the driver of the other significant values we have discussed above. It lights the fire of our lives; it causes an internal revelation and turns our lives in God's direction. It drives our thoughts, aspirations, and behavioral standards.

The Changing Role of Faith and Religion in America

Was America founded as a Christian nation? This is one of the most heated historical debates in America today. On one side, traditional Christians say the founders were Christians and that they built the nation on the principles of faith. On the other side, the secularists argue that the founders were deistic doubters, if not outright atheists; they say the founding was an Enlightenment-inspired, nonreligious event.

In 1775, the Continental Congress "designated a time for prayer in forming a new nation." George Washington proclaimed a day of thanksgiving and prayer in 1795. Lincoln called the nation to prayer at the height of the Civil War, as did Franklin Roosevelt on the eve of D-day in 1944. In 1952 President Harry Truman signed into law the official National Day of Prayer. All these examples of a national focus on prayer were indications that these leaders relied on a "God" for direction and guidance in meeting the challenges of our country.

In the 1830s, the young French nobleman Alexis de Tocqueville traveled throughout the United States, carefully observing its people and institutions. When explaining the success of America's democratic republic to his country-men, he commented at length on the critical role America's lasting religious devotion played. He observed that religion was essential to forming America's democratic "habits of the heart."

Since those very early days of American life, our religious landscape has diversified greatly, and the words of Lincoln have proved to be prophetic.

> But we have forgotten God. We have forgotten the gra-cious hand, which preserved us in peace, and multi-plied and enriched and strengthened us; and we have vainly imagined, in the deceitfulness of our hearts, that all these blessings were produced by some supe-rior wisdom and virtue of our own. Intoxicated with unbroken success, we have become too self-sufficient to feel the necessity of redeeming and preserving grace, too proud to pray to the God that made us.

Diversification and committed secularism have increased significantly, especially in the last fifty years. Consequently, it is fair to ask just how critical faith is for fostering the "habits of the heart" required in a twenty-first-century industrialized democracy. *Deseret News* speaks eloquently to this question: "We believe that, in addition to having con-stitutionally-bound institutions of government, a vibrant democracy requires citizens to obey the law, to address and solve local problems cooperatively, to participate actively in civic life and to behave altruistically. Accordingly, we find that active faith, regardless of denomination, is the best tutor of democratic dispositions. And this is not just our opinion. It is supported by the best contemporary social science."[75]

The erosion of faith in American life continues through the efforts of antifaith groups similar to the Freedom from Religion Foundation. They have a track record of seeking to remove all semblance of God from the public domain. One of their most recent efforts (April 2010) culminated in US District Judge Barbara Crabb's declaration that the National Day of Prayer was unconstitutional. Their hope is that they can parlay their recent victory into a national agenda and rewrite America's spiritual heritage.

The election of the current national administration has exacerbated this debate. The role of gays in the military, homosexual marriage, religious expression in the public square, abortion, and contraception are topics we see mentioned daily in our media. Over the past fifty years we can trace a move toward a more liberal position on these issues. Only through an active insurgency of the "faithful" will this trend be reversed and America's spiritual traditions restored.

The Significance of Faith and Religion

Although there appears to be a trend in American society that could result in public faith being further jeopardized,

---

75 "The Importance of Faith in the Community," *Deseret News*, In Our Opinion, December 19, 2010, http://www.deseretnews.com/article/700092692/The-importance-of-faith-in-the-community.html?pg=all.

we find considerable evidence that faith has had a very powerful, positive impact on our lives. The Bible teaches us that genuine faith is "more precious than gold" (1 Peter 1:7). To be more specific, let's look at recent research that supports the impact of faith on our lives.

Impact on Bodily Health

In her article "Religion and Health," Dr. Gillian Friedman reminds us "that every Jewish service includes recitation of the MiSheBerach, a prayer for those who are ill or recovering from illness or accidents, asks God to assist congregation members in their recovery. Christians invoke God's healing through prayer and fasting. Followers of Hinduism use meditation to heal time sickness, a state of disconnect produced by rushing through life. Virtually every world religion has spiritual remedies to restore mental and physical wellness. Carl Jung, a younger colleague of Sigmund Freud, conceptualized religion as a primordial need of man. Now science confirms that religion and spirituality can have demonstrable health benefits.

According to Dr. Friedman, "Research shows that the comfort and strength gained from religious prayer and spirituality can contribute to healing and a sense of well-being, and can help people cope when confronted with illness and death. Reviews of the medical, psychological and social science literature have shown that people who are motivated by spiritual factors have lower rates of cardiovascular disease, hypertension, obesity, depression, anxiety and gastrointestinal disease. Studies specifically evaluating the impact of religion (rather than broader spirituality) show that, in general, people who are more religious have less psychological distress, depression, suicide, illicit drug use, alcoholism, delinquency and divorce."[76]

David Larson is a senior government researcher in Washington, D.C., and has worked for ten years with the National Institute of Mental Health. His research data tells us that religious people are physically healthier, have fewer heart attacks, and tend to live longer. The religiously committed are less likely to abuse alcohol and use drugs.[77]

Another study, "Why Religion Matters: The Impact of Religious Practice on Social Stability," by the Heritage Foundation, concluded that religion promotes mental health, lessens depression, increases self-esteem, and may aid in recovering from the emotional damage caused by drug and alcohol abuse. Religious practice aids a person's health and tends to increase longevity and prevent disease as well as enhance recovery from disease. The Heritage Foundation research also found that suicide, drug abuse, and out-of-wedlock births are all lessened through the influence of religion.[78]

Unfortunately, religion and faith have only recently been considered important topics for medical and cultural research, and many studies are not methodologically

---

76   Gillian Friedman, "Religion and Health," *Ability Magazine*, accessed January 22, 2013, http://abilitymagazine.com/Health_Religion.html.

77   David Larson, "Effect of Religion on Life," Christian HomeSite, accessed January 22, 2013, http://www.christianhomesite.com/cherryvale/text/effects.htm.

78   Patrick F. Fagan, "Why Religion Matters: The Impact of Religious Practice on Social Stability," The Heritage Foundation, accessed January 25, 1996, http://www.heritage.org/research/reports/1996/01/bg1064nbsp-why-religion-matters.

sophisticated. Nevertheless, many studies similar to those just cited are beginning to separate the specific factors in religious practice that appear to be health related.

Impact on Your Economic Health

In 2003, a *USA Today* article focused on the relationship between religion and wealth. This study revealed that religious affiliation plays a powerful role in how much wealth Americans accumulate, with Jewish people amassing the most and conservative Protestants the least. Mainline Protestants and Catholics fall in between. Moreover, people who attend religious services regularly build more wealth than those who do not.[79]

The effect of religion is robust, even after taking into account inheritance, levels of education, and other factors that may be associated with particular denominations, notes Lisa Keister, associate professor of sociology at Chicago State University. "Religion is an important factor in wealth accumulation that hasn't received a lot of attention in the past," she continues, "but the results suggest people draw on the methods they learn from religion to develop strategies for saving, investing, and spending derived from various faiths."[80]

The Heritage Foundation data also confirms that religious practice tends to move the underprivileged out of poverty and into the middle class. Data from the National Longitudinal Survey of Youth shows that regular church

---

79   "Faith Influences Wealth Accumulation." *USA Today*. December 1, 2003.

80   Ibid.

attendance helps young people escape the poverty of inner-city life. Among youth who attended church regularly, average income was consistently more than 50 percent higher than that of youth who did not practice religious observance. Those who attended religious services in their youth have about $11,000 more in annual income by their early thirties.[81]

Impact on Marital Satisfaction

Marriage and family are sacred and central to most world religions. Even so, until recently many social scientists have regarded religious faith as a relatively minor factor in individual and family development. Minimizing religion is considered justifiable because 95 percent of all married couples and parents in America report a religious affiliation that, for many, consists of little more than a nominal affiliation or occasional attendance at a certain church. Nevertheless, for many, faith profoundly influences both personal and family life.

Larson's research, mentioned earlier, reveals that marital satisfaction tends to increase with church attendance and that religious commitment offers tremendous protection against divorce. People who often attend church are more than twice as likely to remain married. The Heritage Foundation study concluded that church attendance is statistically the most important predictor of marital happiness and stability.[82] In another study, Loren Marks reported that "religious communities, practices and beliefs were of central

---

81   Larson, "Effect of Religion."

82   Ibid.

importance in maintaining, supporting and stabilizing their marriages in the face of time, stress and other challenges."[83]

While it may be true that religion is not an important factor in many American marriages, Miller and Thorsen write in *Spirituality, Religion, and Health: An Emerging Research Field*, "Religion is the single most important influence in [life] for a substantial minority of Americans."[84] Research concludes that regardless of whether you are a believer, there is one truth no one can ignore that is relative to social ills such as crime, drug abuse, alcoholism, family breakdown, sexually transmitted diseases, poverty, or out-of-wedlock births. "Religious belief and practice are demonstrably the strongest social forces against practically any social ill you can name. This is because the real source of all these social ills is simply the absence of God."[85]

University of Virginia sociologist Brad Wilcox concludes, "You do hear, both in Christian and non-Christian circles, that Christians are no different from anyone else when it comes to divorce and that is not true if you are focusing on Christians who are regular church attendees." Wilcox's analysis of National Survey of Families and Households has found that Americans who attend religious services several times a month were about 35 percent less likely to divorce that those with no religious affiliation. In contrast, nominal

---

83   Loren Marks, "How Does Religion Influence Marriage? Christian, Jewish, Mormon, and Muslim Perspective," *Marriage & Family Review* 38, no. 1 (2005): 85–111.

84   W. R. Miller and C. E. Thoresen, "Spirituality, Religion and Health: An Emerging Research Field," *American Psychology*, 58, no. 1 (2003): 24–35.

85   Larson, "Effect of Religion."

evangelicals, who rarely or never attend church, have higher divorce rates than secular couples.[86]

Impact on Parenting

John Bartkowski, a sociologist from Mississippi State University, conducted one of the first studies to examine the impact of religion on the development of young children. His research found that both parents and teachers rated children of parents who regularly attended church services and talked with their children about religion as showing better behavior, self-control, and social skills than children from nonreligious families. Children whose parents both attended church regularly were rated as having the best behavior and being the most well adjusted. Researchers agree that most people who receive Christ as Savior do so when they are children.[87] The message to parents seems clear enough: now is the time for you to invest in your child's coming to faith, and the best place for that to happen is right in your own home. No matter how wonderful church may be, most successful faith launches happen at or near home.

A growing body of empirical research demonstrates that a family's religious involvement directly benefits children, teens, and young adults in a variety of significant ways. In their survey of the research literature, David Dollahite

---

86 Betty Rollin, "Brad Wilcox Extended Interview," *Religion and Ethics Newsweekly*, November 4, 2005, http://www.pbs.org/wnet/religionandethics/episodes/november-4-2005/brad-wilcox-extended-interview/11513/.

87 Gudrun Schultz, "Children Thrive When Parents Follow Religious Beliefs, Study Shows," *LifeSite News*, April 25, 2007, http://www.lifesitenews.com/news/archive//ldn/2007/apr/07042506.

and Jennifer Thatcher found the following benefits from a family's religious involvement:

- Religious practices are linked with family satisfaction and closer parent-child relationships.
- Domestic violence is less among more religious couples, and religious parents are less likely to abuse or yell at their children.
- Religious involvement promotes responsible fathering, and is associated with more involved mothering.[88]

Another study, *The Effective Christian Education: A National Study of Protestant Congregations,* found that family religiousness was the most important factor in faith maturity. It concluded, "Of the two strongest connections to faith maturity, family religiousness is slightly more important than lifetime exposure to Christian education. The particular family experiences that are most tied to greater faith maturity are the frequency with which an adolescent talked with mother and father about faith, the frequency of family devotions, and the frequency with which parents and children together were involved in formal and informal efforts to help each other. Each of these family experiences is more powerful than frequency with which an adolescent sees his or her parents engage in religious behavior like church attendance." The study also found that families who express faith also have an impact on participation in church life and service

88   David C. Dollahite and Jennifer Y. Thatcher, "How Family Religious Involvement Benefits Adults, Youth, and Children" (Salt Lake City, UT: The Sutherland Institute, 2005), http://www.law2.byu.edu/wfpc/forum/2007/Dollahite.pdf.

activities. Twice as many youth in families that express faith are involved in a church youth group, go to church programs or events that include children and adults, go to church camp or work at camp, and regard religious faith as a very important or most important influence in life.[89]

Exercises in Faith

- Listen to the Word of God as much as possible. "Faith comes by hearting and hearing by the word of God" (Rom. 10:17). The book of Proverbs encourages us to constantly keep the Word in our hearts and to keep our attention on it. What we listen to affects what we believe.

- Develop a life of praise and worship. Praise drives away the negativity of your life and brings God into your everyday circumstances. Praising God is an act of faith and helps your faith to grow. God commands it (Heb. 13:15). If you can perceive who God is and see His power, faithfulness, and love, your trust and faith in Him will grow.

- Practice family service. Engaging in service with one's family can be a powerful opportunity to grow in faith. Both children and adults are more likely to have a growing, strong faith when their family serves others together and when children can see their parents' capability, faith, and values in action.

---

89 Peter L. Benson and Carolyn H. Eklin. *The Effective Christian Education: A National Study of Protestant Congregations; A Summary Report on Faith, Loyalty, and Congregational Life* (Minneapolis, MN: Search Institute, 1990): 38.

- Speak the Word. By saying the Word with your mouth, you exercise your faith, you hear the Word, and you build it into your life. Speaking God's Word brings you into the place where God will move to fill the empty spaces of your life.
- Imitate the faith of your spiritual leaders and mentors. Pay special attention to how they attend to the affairs of everyday life. You know people by the way they behave, by the kind of "fruit" they produce. If they are producing good fruit (living right), then consider their ways and follow them (1Cor. 4:15–16; Heb. 13:7).
- Practice faith conversation. Listen and respond to the daily concerns of your family. This kind of conversation can range from supportive listening or sharing the good news of Jesus with another to challenging admonitions from friends or family.
- Filter your life. Sometimes we need to filter a lot of junk that drains our faith out of our lives. When we live a godly life and walk with God, our faith continues to grow. When we walk with our entire minds focused on God and have pure hearts, our faith is bound to grow. If we do not filter out the impurities in our lives, such as fear, doubt, negativity, and unbelief, having faith is hard.
- Recognize family rituals and traditions. Rituals and traditions communicate meaning, values, and relationships that exist between people and God. Family rituals can take many forms, ranging from daily occasions such as mealtime, bedtime, to celebrations such as birthdays, anniversaries, and special achievements.

- Do something. Don't just sit there and expect your Christian walk to be vibrant and "on fire." Reach out and prioritize your life and commitments so that you are receiving or being around Christian values and influence.
- Spend as much time as you can with people of faith. Their spirit of faith will touch your life (Prov. 13:20).

CHAPTER 11

A New Beginning

When I stand before God at the end of my life, I would hope that I would not have a single bit of talent left, and could say, "I used everything you gave me."

— ERMA BOMBECK

We began this journey with a quote from Elwyn Brooks White, which highlighted the daily challenge of whether our lives are committed to "improving" or "enjoying" the world. Most of us wake up each day with a desire for some level of success. And while our idea of what success looks like may vary from individual to individual, no one wakes up every morning wanting to be a failure. However we define "success," we identify certain goals we believe will define us and our efforts. After we achieve those goals and are considered a success, then what do we do? Do we just continue to add new goals and pursue them as aggressively as we did the previous ones? We can begin to see the endless cycle that characterizes most of our lives if we focus primarily on success and give little thought to significance.

Nothing is wrong with pursuing success. On the contrary, we applaud those who discipline themselves, create goals for themselves, and achieve success. Isn't that the American dream? But almost all the goals we pursue for success have one thing in common: they all die when we die. Success may be achieving a promotion, lowering your golf handicap, achieving sales-manager-of-the-year status, or becoming president of the local service club. All these marks of success eventually rust out, are destroyed, deteriorate, are discarded, or just lose their appeal. Very few of these successes last.

That small, almost unnoticed line — the dash — engraved on our tombstones between the dates of our birth and death has lost its significance. In fact, on some tombstones the dash is completely eliminated, almost suggesting that the person's life was characterized only by a birthday and the day of our death. On the other hand, a dash of significance leaves a legacy if we can invest our lives in others to perpetuate them beyond our lifetimes. Significance demands that we take the focus off our own pursuits, accomplishments, and possessions and identify ways in which we can leverage our success for the good of others. Significance requires that we somehow use every award, special recognition, and honor we receive as a platform to share lessons of empowerment with others. But above all, significance requires that we leave this earth a little better place than when we entered it, more enriched because we took the time to leave a lasting legacy by sharing with others what we have learned.

In these pages, I have shared with you eight values that were at least significant in my life. These values have guided the direction of my steps, and as I have experienced their impact on my life, I have attempted to share them with others who have accompanied me on my dash — sharing, encouraging, and directing the lives of our children, especially our grandchildren. I have always believed that as long as our children call me Dad, I have the responsibility, diminishing though it is with age, to monitor and guide them, to be a role model for them, and to leave them a legacy of significance. My daily challenge is not only to adapt these eight values into my own life but also to leave this legacy to our children and to their children — and the beat goes on.

As I suggested above, these values may not be yours, but I encourage you to seek out the values that give meaning to your own life. One of my first challenges each day is to wander out on our small condo patio. We have only two potted plants, but I enjoy their beauty. I pick off the wilted leaves and petals, give the plants a fresh drink of water, fertilize them, rearrange them to maximize the rays of sun they will receive during the day, and then just sit back and enjoy them.

God encourages us to live our "dash" in this same tender, loving, and mindful way, taking the days God has given us and making them meaningful and significant.

As we read about and listen to what is happening around the world each day, it is very easy to let the noise of the negative minority drown out the steady sound of the good that is all around us. I truly believe in the goodness of most people, and they probably deserve more credit than we are willing to give them. Our challenge, however, is that the good we are doing doesn't always represent our best. In our quieter moments we sense that too often our lives are pointed in the direction of success, usually personal success, with little regard to whether we have built significance in them.

My spouse is quick to classify a good dinner at our favorite restaurant as "excellent." My retort is that "excellent" leaves little or no room for improvement. Aren't our lives a little like this? I usually feel a persisting desire to stretch my life by looking for worthy ways to make more of a difference in my own life and in the lives of my family, of my community, and, in some small way, even of the world.

My goal in sharing the thoughts expressed in this book is to attempt to inspire you to lead a more significant life, to give you the nudge that refocuses your life on the type of legacy you will leave, and to prod you to be the "'transition" person who will cause the lives of those around you to become significant. They, in turn, will foster this transition from generation to generation or from situation to situation, whether in a family, the workplace, the community, or even beyond.

In mentoring my children and grandchildren, I have often used the image of life being like a corked bottle on the seas, flowing passively with the action of the waves, in comparison with a life in which we are proactive and take responsibility for our actions, acting upon our lives rather than allowing life to act upon us. But, of course, none of this happens by chance; it happens only if we live in harmony with many of the values set forth earlier. The associated research cited in each chapter suggests that using these values can be instrumental in mobilizing our lives toward greater well-being and significance.

So are you ready? Ready to give life, significant life, to the dash that will one day separate the dates of your birth and death? Are you ready to clarify what your life will stand for and how you will pursue it? I ask:

- Are you practicing the universal values outlined in this book?
- Is your life similar to a corked bottle, being tossed to and fro?
- To what ends are your daily choices leading?

If you are unsure of your answers, reread the exercises at the end of each chapter. The outcome of each exercise will be a reminder that you have the potential for significance— don't let it pass you by!

Too many people live with regret, missed opportunities, and dormant dreams. Is that your legacy? Your life provides you with the opportunity to choose how you will spend your dash. Are you living the dash, knowing fully who you are and why you are here? Or are you dashing to live, hurriedly spending precious time chasing things that really don't matter? The psalmist prayed, "Teach us to number our days and recognize how few they are, help us to spend them as we should" (Ps. 90:12).

It's never too late to improve your dash. In *Game Plan*, Bob Buford reminds us, "If you were a machine, it would be called 'retrofitting' — making some adjustments in the original piece of equipment so that it can perform new tasks. If you were a piece of software, it would be called 'upgrading' — same basic package, but with new revisions and new features that keep it on the cutting edge."[90] Richard Capen, in his book *Finish Strong*, calls improving your dash "repotting."[91] Whatever improving your dash is called, it is a renaissance — your personal opportunity to make your life more significant.

Do you remember your days of building sand castles at the beach? How you would sit for hours, digging and smoothing, trying to get every aspect just right? Then the tide would begin to roll in, causing the waves to creep higher and higher and gradually wash away your castle. It took several attempts before you realized your sand castles were not permanent — they couldn't last.

Unfortunately, too often we end up feeling the same way at the end of our lives. We've worked an overscheduled life, and eventually our aging bodies slow us down, and we look at what we struggled to construct. The harsh reality we often face is that much of what we strove for won't last. After we die it will wash away like a sand castle at high tide. In *One Month to Live*, the authors suggest that if we had just

90   Bob Buford, *Game Plan: Winning Strategies for the Second Half of Your Life* (Grand Rapids, MI: Zondervan, 1997), 22.

91   Richard Capen, *Finish Strong: Living the Values That Take You the Distance* (San Francisco: Zondervan, 1996), 48.